REALIGNING FOR CHANGE

8 Principles for Successful Change Management in Your Organization

David Molden and Jon Symes

FINANCIAL TIMES
PITMAN PUBLISHING

FINANCIAL TIMES
MANAGEMENT

LONDON • SAN FRANCISCO
KUALA LUMPUR • JOHANNESBURG

*Financial Times Management delivers the knowledge,
skills and understanding that enable students,
managers and organisations to achieve their ambitions,
whatever their needs, wherever they are.*

London Office:
128 Long Acre, London WC2E 9AN
Tel: +44 (0)171 447 2000
Fax: +44 (0)171 240 5771
Website: www.ftmanagement.com

A Division of Financial Times Professional Limited

First published in Great Britain in 1999

© Financial Times Professional Limited 1999

The right of David Molden and Jon Symes to be identified as authors
of this work has been asserted by them in accordance
with the Copyright, Designs and Patents Act 1988.

ISBN 0 273 63381 3

British Library Cataloguing in Publication Data
A CIP catalogue record for this book can be obtained from the British Library.

10 9 8 7 6 5 4 3 2 1

Typeset by Northern Phototypesetting Co, Ltd.
Printed and bound in Great Britain by Bell & Bain Ltd, Glasgow

The Publishers' policy is to use paper manufactured from sustainable forests.

About the authors

Dave Molden Born and educated in the UK, Dave first learned how to facilitate success among people by managing teams in the information technology industry. This experience led to a role directing training and development activities in one of the UK's fastest growing and most successful service companies, Computacenter.

Always looking for creative and more effective ways of developing people, Dave has become something of an expert in challenging orthodoxy. He is author of *Managing with the Power of NLP*, a self-help book for managers which continues to receive worldwide acclaim. Dave is a director with CPS International.

Jon Symes Born and educated in the UK, Jon has a background in international business with ICI. He is well-renowned for his coaching and development work in helping people to realise their innate talents to the fullest. Jon has a unique ability to distill ideas and simplify processes, bringing clarity to the most complex of situations.

Jon is driven by the desire to help others become more successful. He is in demand from a growing number of leading organisations to support key people and bring innovation to their most difficult business challenges. Jon is a director with CPS International.

Together the authors are committed to creating an environment in their own company that other organisations strive for. It is their belief in the principles of alignment that are enabling them to achieve this, driven on by values of eduction, creativity, innovation and success. As consultants, facilitators, trainers and coaches they have worked with many organisations including Nestlé, HM Customs and Excise, Computacenter, Marks & Spencer Financial Services, Philip Morris Inc., BICC, Littlewoods, and the Institute of Management.

Contents

Acknowledgements

We gratefully acknowledge the people without whom we may not have developed the insight or motivation to begin this project, including the people who have done so much to develop the concept of alignment: Gregory Bateson for the original insight and Robert Dilts who has developed and embroidered that insight in many ways; those people who have taught us so many other related ideas which have joined this stream of thought: Dr Wyatt Woodsmall, Marvin Oka and Richard Diehl deserve a large amount of thanks here.

To all of the other teachers, clients, colleagues and friends who have helped us along this path of learning: you are too many to mention by name but we trust you will recognise our sincere gratitude. To our colleagues at CPS International for their enthusiastic co-operation and encouragement, most particularly to Sharon Friere for her support. To Ray Perkins for his logic, reasoning and attention to detail in proofing the earlier work. To Pradeep Jethi and the team at Financial Times Management for their enthusiasm and faith in our ideas. Finally, and most important, to our wives and children for their support and tolerance of all of the weekends and evenings spent putting our thoughts, ideas and experiences into words.

We're glad it's finished too.

Introduction

What the book is about

Some books purport to reveal great lessons for managers and leaders in organisations. This book can do that, and more. Alignment is a new concept, never before presented to the business world. It consists of some powerful new thinking which is capable of producing shifts of real significance in any organisation. The consequences of assimilating these fundamental ideas will be far greater than anything yet experienced from a methodology or technique. We want our readers to create an ethos for sustainable success.

We have two major contributions to make to management thinking, of that we are confident. First, we provide fresh insights into the key issues that businesses are facing today. For example, our ideas address organisational change by moving the debate into a new realm where change is not a lurking monster, to be fought with and defeated before we return to our steady-state operating. Instead, we open up a paradigm of change as a constant, as a friend, an opportunity for continuous improvement of the quality and effectiveness of our operations. Managing change is one of the four key themes we have chosen in our treatment of the alignment concept, which, reflecting on our experience in a number of leading organisations, we recognise as crucial elements to sustainable success. The remaining three themes are innovation, teamworking and leadership.

Innovation is increasingly sought as the answer to gaining a competitive edge. We believe that innovation is central to the fabric of all organisations – the difference between those at the front of the field and those at the rear will be the degree by which innovation has been integrated into the culture. We provide you with the thinking to unlock innovation in your organisation. We share with you the key factors which act to inhibit innovation, and we guide you in the practical steps to stimulate it. Behind that we promise you will find the attitudes that successful innovators use to support their success.

Teams are vital building blocks. If they consist of individuals aligned with one another, and if they are aligned with the goals of the organisation, then the fullest potential of your workforce can be deployed. We have refined and distilled the art of building teams such that it is highly usable, providing clear and simple guidelines for growing high performance teams. One of the teams we have had the pleasure of working with over the years recently presented its departing leader with a classy, top brand wristwatch. It wasn't so much the impressive business growth and performance the team wished to recognise. This gift came from the heart, as a sincere thank you for the journey of personal growth and development, and the team spirit he had helped them to create. That leader had used, and role modelled for his team, the principles which you will find between these pages.

The topic of leadership is a priority for organisations wanting to take and maintain a lead in the marketplace. Leadership is the motive force in any enterprise, shaping the climate for the utilisation of human energy. We give you a different perspective on this subject, one which reveals the most important focus for your development investment – defining leadership to release the true creative potential of the workforce.

The second contribution we make to management thinking is to have ventured far beyond the conventional recipe for improvement. This is more than a step-by-step guide to improvements or a simple ten-point plan. Our book represents a tour of the fundamental mechanics of performance for people in organisations. The universal alignment model shows us where to place our attention in order to get the results we want. This book will provide you with a new language which you can use to analyse the parameters of performance and design improvements.

The most lasting benefit of the ideas herein is that they show you how to understand the fundamental components of performance and success. The ideas will help you become aligned – with whatever you want. So you become your own guide and developer, knowing what to pay attention to, and how to design the changes you want. This information is not about specific changes. It is not for those who want to tinker with systems. Rather, it contains a level of generic thought which will leave you self-reliant, whatever your field of endeavour.

The scope of application for alignment thinking is broad. The concept works for any system, including groups, small local workteams, or the teams that make up organisations of any size or shape. And if we consider the individual as a system too, we have a book with insights as relevant to personal development as to organisational development. The threads of application ideas running through the book have been carefully crafted to include reference to both ends of this size spectrum and all points in between.

We have drawn upon our consulting experience with organisations big and small. Indeed, it is this experience which has persuaded us of the value and versatility of alignment as a concept. We use it as we consider interventions to help companies respond at corporate level to their latest challenges. We use it when coaching to select the most effective points of leverage, thus enabling people to make changes that better support their aspirations. We use it to facilitate groups and to design training interventions. It is roadtested and proven as a concept – we know it works. We have played back as many anecdotes and stories to enrich your reading most usefully. These are all true accounts of actual events and so, in most cases, we have made them anonymous.

Just as our experience spans all types of organisations, big, small, public and private sectors, this book is intended for all of those audiences. We have endeavoured to make this clear in the text by referring to 'organisations'. Where we have talked instead of businesses, or companies, it is to prevent overusing the word and is not meant to imply any limitation on the application of the ideas. Similarly, we have tried to distribute our gender references equally, for we know that the ideas have resonance for all of us.

Meanings

We use the words 'conscious' and 'unconscious' to make important distinctions. Unconscious refers to the thinking that occurs at a deeper level than our immediate awareness. This type of thinking controls habitual behaviour, that is, we don't have to think about how to do something, we just do it. Conscious refers to thinking at a much higher level of awareness and alertness. Driving a car provides an example of both. While the controls of the car can be adequately operated unconsciously, without having to think about it, we are consciously thinking about other vehicles, traffic signs, landmarks, road signs and other important information.

The word 'system' can mean anything comprising interrelated components having an input, a process and an output. We have applied the term to a human being, a team, an organisation or any component part of it.

How the book came about

Our purpose in writing this book is to make the alignment approach available to others so that organisations will change for the better. A workplace can be an oasis of life where people thrive, willingly giving their energy and commitment to a worthy cause. They can be places where success is celebrated frequently, and where people are free to express their full potential. Yet all too often they succeed in suppressing energy and alienating commitment. Writing this book has allowed us to pull together all our experience with many different organisations, and to draw from it the essence of success. We want it to work for you.

How to use the book

We have endeavoured to present alignment not as a set of academic theories or collection of ideas, but in practical terms, drawing upon our experience, and from those we have learned from over the years. Alignment works – we were convinced of that many years ago. The liberal inclusion of audit questionnaires and other simple devices will, we hope, entice you to reflect widely on your own situations at work, and we encourage you to try out some of our ideas with your team, and others in your organisation. Try out the approaches in your workplace and call us to let us know the results you get. We would like to hear from you.

Layout

We have paid particular attention to the layout of the book, wanting to make the material memorable and easy to read. We hope the signposts we have used will help you to identify sections you find particularly useful, and make reference easier.

Key

 An alignment icon is used to indicate a **principle**.

 A pen icon is used to indicate **how to** do something. This may be a checklist of pointers, some relevant questions, or an audit questionnaire.

 A light bulb icon accompanies a **quote** used for extra emphasis.

 Anecdotes are set in grey panels.

Part 1

ALIGNMENT EXPLAINED

1

ALIGNMENT

Introduction

One of the most vivid images of alignment I have seen is a photograph by George Silk published by Time-Life. The shot captures perfectly the moment when Kathy Flicker, a diver, enters the water, half in and half out, absolutely vertical, straight-bodied and poised. In diving, alignment of this quality is scored very highly, indeed the diver's goal is to enter the water in exactly this fashion, having completed a particular movement through the air.

Diving also provides us with an important insight into success. Wyatt Woodsmall, who worked as a coach with the US diving team during the 1980s, related how Greg Louganis, the late American diver, world champion and winner of four Olympic gold medals used a two-step process to beat the world.

An Olympic diving pool has water jets directed onto the surface of the pool underneath the diving board. This helps divers to gauge their height above the water surface. Without the spray pattern rippling across the surface the divers on the high board can find it difficult to know where the water level is.

During his flight through the air on each dive Louganis would pay attention to the sound of these jets, only faint from the 10-metre board, more easily discerned as he dived, and loudest at water level. Louganis was then able to modify his movement through the air according to the position he was at, calculated from this sound. Other divers, it seems, were unable to make this distinction. Without the information gained from this input other equally acrobatic divers would go through their complex airborne manoeuvres aiming to straighten up at the right time to knife cleanly into the water. The advantage that Louganis had was the twin-fold ability to make a particular distinction in the information his senses were picking up during his flight, and then to respond accordingly.

This great sportsman demonstrated that to excel at any particular activity we need only know two things. First, we must learn the key distinctions to which we should pay attention. Second, we need to develop strategies that incorporate the information from these distinctions to modify our performance. When learning a foreign language emphasis is put on learning the grammar, structure and vocabulary, while one of the key distinctions often missed is the rhythm of the language. Learning the rhythm enhances the speed at which a language is learned. With access to useful distinctions and some strategies to help us respond to the information gained we can systematically improve our performance in any area we choose.

> The universal alignment model shows us the key distinctions we can pay attention to in systems in order to improve performance.

The universal alignment model shows us the key distinctions we can pay attention to in systems in order to improve performance. The model has equal validity for any system, be it a team, a company or a human being. Attention to these specific distinctions, plus some effective strategies to make use of the information gained, can help us to deal with an enormous number of situations, including many of the most common and the most vexed problems facing organisations today. Let us introduce the universal alignment model and its key distinctions and discuss these in the context of that most simple of questions – what do we want?

The universal alignment model

There are six key distinctions which can be identified, analysed and purposefully aligned to optimise output (see Figure 1.1). Some of these alignment distinctions are well-known – already part of the business language, they are regularly and consciously used. Action, for example, is measured, targeted and developed in quite sophisticated ways in organisations. As individuals we have a pretty clear idea what our capabilities are. Other distinctions we are discussing in this book are less apparent and much less well-used. Few people, for example, give conscious thought to their sense of identity. Few organisations try to capture the beliefs and unwritten rules that govern the decisions and actions of employees. Sometimes, like the earlier example of rhythm and language, distinctions are overlooked, either for reasons of ignorance, expedition or perhaps low priority. This can result in reduced efficiency, ineffectiveness, dysfunction or worse.

Whether for individuals, teams or for whole organisations we can examine any one of these distinctions and gauge how it relates to any other. In the following chapters we show how these distinctions can become the levers for change in any system. We explore, in a variety of ways, how to align the system by using these levers. Let us look at each in turn.

> **Our purpose is our reason for being.**

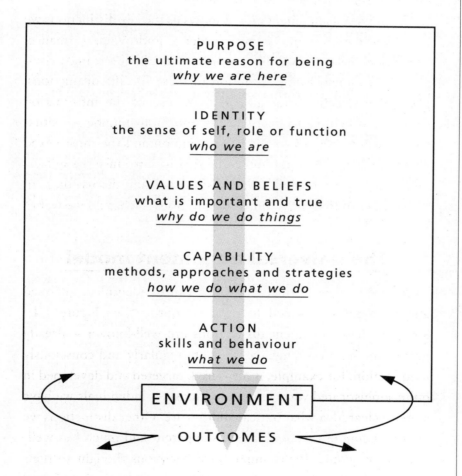

**Figure 1.1
Universal
alignment
model**

■ Purpose

Our purpose is our reason for being. At an individual level we have a purpose. We come together in groups with purpose, indeed groups dissolve if there is no purpose in being together. Purpose serves as a direction, a constant that we can refer to over time.

This does not mean that purpose is always obvious or recognisable. Indeed, within many organisations there can be people who are genuinely uncertain why the organisation exists. Often purpose is insufficiently articulated for people to identify the link between collective purpose and their own efforts. If people identify strongly with some team, site or function within the organisation that has a clear purpose their need might be met. Without even this there is an immediate waste of energy as people labour without the fullest information by which to judge the significance of their effort.

Some people are very clear about their own individual purpose in life. It comes as no surprise to find that many of these are engaged in what we regard as vocational work: following their vocation, their calling, their purpose. For others, the question of purpose seldom arises and when it does it is quickly put away unanswered, maybe even as unanswerable. One of the features of modern life when so many of our simple survival needs are catered for is the searching for purpose. A number of the people we work with as clients and some friends in middle life find this question of purpose difficult to answer, and we observe how disorienting this can be in many different ways. Life purpose can be a beacon. It can help us navigate through our time on this planet. Without such a landmark to give us a reference, constant over time, individual issues and daily decisions become more stressful.

> This is the true joy in life, the being used for a purpose recognised by yourself as a mighty one ... the being a force of nature instead of a feverish, selfish little clod of ailments and grievances complaining that the world will not devote itself to making you happy.
> [George Bernard Shaw]

> One of the features of modern life when so many of our simple survival needs are catered for is the searching for purpose.

> Life purpose can be a beacon.

■ Identity

Our sense of self has enormous moment in our lives but is often only expressed unconsciously. Our sense of self is the answer to the question 'Who are you?' Few people hold their thoughts on this readily formed, nor is this highly personal subject often broached. The response, were we asked this question, would likely consist of our name, and perhaps a job or organisational title. And when asked to talk about ourselves, our own self, many of us respond in terms of what we do and where we live or work.

The ablest man I ever met is the man you think you are. [Franklin D Roosevelt]

To illustrate the importance of this particular aspect of our thoughts, consider the different behaviours you might expect from a traffic policeman and an inspirational leader of nations. Perhaps they don't seem related to each other very strongly. Not so for Wolfgang, who wondered why he found it difficult to engage with his team in his new job. He likened his middle management role to that of a traffic cop standing on a podium at the centre of a busy intersection. Not much real dialogue with the passing motorists was possible, he concluded, and this way of thinking was not moving him towards his outcome of productive enjoyable teamwork. Improvements followed quickly upon his redefinition of his identity. He reconstructed this around the role of a compassionate and inspiring leader, a simple pattern of thinking that combined the interaction and cross-fertilisation he wished to experience with his team.

In groups the sense of identity is equally important.

A couple of years ago we worked with a company supplying on-site IT services for a customer. Many of the 20-strong team thought of themselves as a help desk, there to solve problems for the customer's employees. Fixing problems was the extent of their involvement: job done, return to base and wait for the next problem to crop up and be solved. The team's manager knew that customer needs were changing and the contract was up for renewal. She knew that the customer wanted a partnership, in which the supplier's IT expertise was put at the disposal of the customer's staff. Adding this kind of value to the customer's business would require a very different set of responses on call-out.

'That problem's fixed, can I do anything else to help you or to speed up some of your routine tasks on the PC? What do you use it for anyway? Have you got the hardware and software you need?'

Had the team been able to adopt that new identity and the behaviours it generated more quickly, the contract might have been saved.

It is necessary to the happiness of man that he be mentally faithful to himself. Infidelity does not consist in believing, or in disbelieving, it consists in professing to believe what one does not believe.
[Tom Paine, *The Age of Reason*]

■ Values and beliefs

Values are those things we hold as most important. As such they, too, influence our behaviour. Values become apparent quite readily in conversation and can usually be discussed more easily than identity. Indeed, in recent years some organisations have brought values firmly onto the corporate agenda. A statement of company values is a common sight on the wall in reception nowadays and many of us will have taken part in debates about what is important to us in our work.

Values are abstract concepts like integrity, service, professionalism or quality. To help us to put these into operation we construct our own rules or interpretations of these values in the form of beliefs. So someone who values open communication might believe this can be accomplished through wandering around the workplace frequently. Another person might believe that listening before speaking is helpful in specific situations. Perhaps providing access to information on a computer intranet is another person's interpretation of the same value. Ask any team to list its beliefs attached to this value and you are likely to get many additional interpretations. So values spawn beliefs and these in turn influence our choice of behaviour.

Values are those things we hold as most important.

An organisation's values might tell us something about what the upper echelons want to be reflected in the behaviour of all employees. But unless these values are in place and the process of translating them into behaviour is well-attended to, the results might differ from the intention.

> This reminds us of one company for whom we have worked. We had some ideas to help people identify the organisation's key values and to use them throughout the various functions. Unfortunately for us, another consultancy was employed to help the top team with this same thinking. Many mandays of retreat and reflection followed before the fruit of this labour was ready, printed and circulated. Sadly, the end result was a list of about 20 values, a veritable shopping list of corporate virtue, and well beyond the ability of anyone, even those involved, to memorise and use.

Values need translation if they are to be more than intention. And if we want to compare intention and execution we should look to the culture that we encounter in any organisation, as it is the best indicator of the prevalent values in that workforce.

Values need translation if they are to be more than intention.

■ Capability

Imagine a newborn baby. It is an enormous privilege to be present as a new life is brought into this world, and my two experiences of this reinforced for me a belief that underpins all of our work. Human beings have an extraordinary capability to do and to achieve so many things. Holding a baby makes me think about the inherent human capabilities, to be loving, intelligent, energetic and resourceful, to enjoy life and to enjoy co-operative relationships with others. It is useful to assume this to be true, to work

**If you can dream it, you can do it.
[Walt Disney]**

from this position and to figure out and remove anything that has acted to close down that innate capability. Because closed down it is, to a greater or lesser degree, in all of us. We operate so far below the levels of our true potential, encumbered as we are with the accumulated conditioning and patterns of behaviour that can be so difficult to break.

> **Human beings have an extraordinary capability to do and to achieve so many things.**

Capability is about potential. Our focus in this book, and indeed in all of our consulting work, is on removing the blockages that prevent people from fulfilling their potential and finding ways of helping people to access their innate resources. We have learned, through our consulting experience, and through the pursuit of our own personal development, that alignment is vital to increasing capability in individuals, teams and organisations.

■ Action

> **The chains of habit are too weak to be felt until they are too strong to be broken. [Dr Samuel Johnson]**

At both team and individual level it is action which is the visible and tangible output. It can usually be measured, directed and developed, so it is no surprise that managers want to influence action to get favourable performance results. If the cause–effect can be that simple we only need to worry about this one lever in order to manage output and to manage change.

Of course, it is not this simple, but action remains one of the important factors we want to consider in our alignment. Quality of action depends upon the deliberate application of a systematic method of tracking and achieving the tasks set before us. Indeed, the phrase performance management refers to any systematic way of allocating tasks between the people in the group and measuring their progress towards achieving those tasks. Most enterprises have some such system for controlling and co-ordinating how people's actions are applied.

But another aspect of action is the unconscious, unguarded behaviour we exhibit as human beings. So much of what we do is outside the realms of conscious choice that we are frequently revealing our thoughts, feelings or attitude in behaviour of which we are not even aware. What, for instance, is the look on your face as you talk to your colleagues at work? Feelings, whether of tiredness, enthusiasm or other emotions, are sometimes not easily hidden and the signs are evident in body posture, gesture and facial expression. So when we think of action we need to bear in mind what unintentional behaviour we might engage in.

> **Our intention and others' interpretation of our action are often worlds apart.**

We worked with a director of a publicly quoted company who cared deeply about creating an environment in which people felt respected, worthwhile and happy. As a confident, even laid-back presenter, he was quite shocked to think that his practice of addressing senior management team meetings without a rigorous preparation or a rehearsal might itself appear to the team as lacking in respect. While we are fully conscious of many aspects of our action and its impact on others, there are some occasions when we are less so. Our intention, and others' interpretation of our action are often worlds apart.

■ Environment

The environment influences us individually and in groups in a number of ways. Let us give you a personal example.

Man's character is the product of his premises. [Ayn Rand]

In our own business we are currently realising a number of benefits from a recent office move. Our previous accommodation was somewhat cramped, unattractive and not conducive to creative and exciting work. We certainly didn't invite our clients to meet us there. In contrast, the new office has space, views over open countryside and some new, more comfortable furnishings. Since moving, colleagues have talked about their increased enthusiasm for their jobs and we've noticed some different effects on other people. We now use these attractive premises as part of our offer to customers; we invite them in to see us and our meetings are so much more enjoyable and productive. Aligning our working environment to the value we put on creativity and people has borne fruit already.

Even from this simple illustration it can be seen that the environment is one of the factors that needs to be aligned with others in order that desired outcomes are achieved. This includes the physical environment such as rooms and decor, comfortable furnishings and lighting. We can also think of the equipment, tools and information we have, indeed almost any tangible resources required to assist the job, including funding. Providing the budget might be part of setting the right environment for success.

Our environment affects every other one of the alignment distinctions in some way.

The universal model we illustrated and described in Figure 1.1 shows environment as one of these important distinctions. It also demonstrates another very important factor about our environment. Our environment affects every other one of the alignment distinctions in some way. Each of these factors is, to an important degree, a reaction to the context in which the system exists.

The environment, or context, of the system will influence the key factors of attitude, namely identity, values and beliefs. Think of this in personal terms. It is our own perception of our situation which determines which identity we assume. Generally speaking, between the hours of 9 and 5 on weekdays we perceive our context as that of 'work' and we assume our working identity with its accompanying values and belief structures.

In a different perceived context our identity might shift to that of Mum, Dad, lover or friend. Each different context in which we operate can trigger changes in our thinking patterns. These may be subtle shifts in the values we apply in our different roles, giving greater emphasis to particular core values at work or at home. For other people, these can be wholly separate paradigms in which a very different persona is apparent. The quiet work colleague becomes a more confident and extravert individual in their own social environment.

For organisations, the perception of context is just as important in determining the stance to adopt. The purpose and identity chosen will be and should be a response to the world in which that organisation is operating, or at least the world in which its people perceive it to be operating. Consider the public sector in the UK, and how the context perceived by senior managers is one in which priorities shift rapidly and ultimate decision-making authority rests with the political masters of the day. The resulting identities adopted by these senior people can be markedly different from those seen among their private sector peers, the former aware of the restraining hand on the reins, the latter oozing initiative and self-determination. Both are managers, but their perceptions of context are vastly different, and so, therefore, are their distinctions across the entire universal alignment model.

Our environment, in part fashioned by our own actions, is a context in which we form our particular thoughts and words and deeds. It deserves our attention.

So what do you want?

This is an important question, but is one which often gets forgotten. So, we have this idea of alignment, and therefore we must ask what we want from being aligned. Let us use the word outcomes to describe what we want. Using this word, rather than goals or objectives, allows us to think differently, in a new and clearer way about our desires. Goals, targets and objectives are words which have a ring of aspiration about them, the possibility of success brings its companion, the possibility of failure. Outcome, however, means simply the product of our behaviour. We use the word with a clear link established in our minds: our actions will have outcomes, there will be outcomes.

Outcomes are a great yardstick.

This is as true for companies as for teams or individual human beings. Our challenge, therefore, is to think about our intended outcomes in such a way as to ensure that they do indeed materialise.

Outcomes are a great yardstick. We can use them to measure the success of the endeavour of any of the systems we are considering. Thinking about how to achieve the outcomes that motivate us allows us to see the contribution of the other distinctions in the alignment model. We can analyse each of these in terms of how they support the achievement of our outcomes.

For example, if I run a business and set a goal to achieve 50 percent increase in turnover by a variety of sales and marketing strategies, that is what people will focus on – a future goal. This is useful, but even more useful and effective is to consider having successfully achieved your goal and then imagine the outcomes that stem from this, for example, more people doing different things, a bigger operation, a more complex business, more enthusiasm, a higher cost base, a new team.

So what difference does this make? Using outcomes covers more ground and gives a more systemic focus on strategies. It encourages you to step into the reality of your achievements, working 'as if' you already have them. It also allows you to consider more of the consequences of a strategy including those outside the environment of the organisation as well as those within it (look again at Figure 1.1). Companies are in the public eye like never before with media coverage of the best and worst performing companies. A reputation outside the organisation as a bad employer can have a devastating effect on the inside. So we are encouraging you to think of outcomes when you are deciding what it is that you want.

What is alignment?

So when a system is aligned, these six factors – identity, values and beliefs, capability, action and environment – are aligned with one another. Let us take two examples that demonstrate this.

Imagine an organisation whose fundamental purpose is clear and understood by all. Every member of the organisation has been able to take a conscious choice to support that purpose in accepting his position in the first place and in retaining it thereafter. There will be a consistent understanding of the organisation's identity across the workforce, and of the role the company plays for its customers, business partners and staff. No one will be expecting the organisation to provide for them in ways other than those contracted, as broadly or narrowly as these are stated. The values and culture are an umbrella ensuring the achievement of the outcomes. They accommodate different opinions and preferences among employees in a positive combination. The actions taken by the organisation and the people within it will support its outcomes with sufficient flexibility to deal with change. All of this will happen within a conducive environment. The expected outcomes become actual results quickly and efficiently.

A person who is aligned is one who knows her purpose in life, and who has found an identity or role in which she can advance toward this. Her values will support her in the identity chosen and her beliefs will enable her to move towards the desired outcome. Beliefs that disempower or distract will have been identified and countered. This person will do what needs to be done and in the way in which it needs doing to adapt her immediate environment to support success. She will have the motivation and flexibility to move efficiently towards her outcomes.

The desired condition is that of being aligned. In this condition energy flows naturally and easily to where it is most needed.

Actions taken are those most likely to lead to the outcomes desired. There is no 'internal friction' to be overcome.

Oriental health systems provide a good analogy here. In contrast to western medicine which thinks mostly in terms of removing disease or reducing dysfunction, oriental thinking focuses on the desired outcome, good health. The Chinese and Indian systems have one thing in common: both recognise the importance of energy and its flow in the body. Different mechanisms are used to promote energy flow. The yogic word for regulated breathing, pranayama, is built around the root, *prana*, which means life force or vital energy. The Chinese will practice the movement of chi, energy, through disciplines such as tai-chi and chi kung. In both systems there is progress toward a condition in which energy can circulate easily and be used most efficiently. This, we believe, mirrors our goal both corporately and individually. Alignment is achievable through attention to the six factors described.

> The desired condition is that of being aligned. In this condition energy flows naturally and easily to where it is most needed.

What is misalignment?

We are tuned to detect misalignment in other people. Our senses pick up when someone else's actions appear at odds with their words. Sometimes when we cannot be more precise, we talk of having a 'gut feeling' about someone. This is incongruence, a misalignment spotted when performance is not aligned with one or more other factors. The clues that betray this are usually non-verbal, unconscious actions. You will be able to recall times when you knew someone was being dishonest, or did not really agree with what they declared to be a good idea. What was it that told you: a look on their face, a shifting posture or a wringing of hands? Students of body language will know that there is a high correlation between asymmetry and incongruence. In other words, the metaphorical misalignment is made visible as a postural misalignment which holds the body or facial expression in a non-symmetrical pose.

On a group scale, the clues about misalignment need a wider range of view to spot, but they are there nonetheless. Misalignment is antagonism towards or friction between people. So when we detect lasting disharmony, long-term disagreements or people working against their better judgement we have misalignment. There is nothing new in finding these symptoms of friction undesirable. But treating them as the misalignments they are allows us to remedy the situation. There is, further, a difference between misalignment and disagreement. Vigorous debate and opposing ideas can be a healthy way of making decisions. Misalignment occurs when opposing ideas become opposing beliefs that are fixed and work against the common good. This is an important distinction to watch for. A congruent shift in ideas often requires a change in belief.

On a corporate scale, we need a still wider range of view to spot misalignment. Indeed, we also need to know what it is that would tell us the organisation was not aligned. Here, culture is the truest indicator. Sir John Harvey-Jones, former Chairman of ICI and now famous TV troubleshooter, would boast of being able to assess a company's state of well-being by sampling the culture. His preferred method for doing this was a visit to the shopfloor or its equivalent. It is here, away from the smooth phrases and platitudes of the boardroom that the alignment between corporate aspiration and daily physical endeavour could best be judged. The culture, detectable on such a visit, will reveal to what extent individuals support the outcomes of the organisation. It will show how the declared corporate values are actually being role modelled by the most senior managers. Do they walk their talk?

> **Culture may be viewed as the rules, norms and attitudes that are commonly found among those engaged in any joint activity.**

Culture may be viewed as the rules, norms and attitudes that are commonly found among those engaged in any joint activity. As such it provides an incontrovertible feedback to the leaders about how well the individuals are aligned with the organisation. Much talk circulates about culture change, consultants and gurus offering different remedies and approaches. Yet, in a sense, the culture of an organisation is akin to the wake left by an ocean liner. The wake will reflect the rate and direction of the vessel's progress through the water. The wake is not permanent and cannot be captured. It exists over time but is actually being created and is decaying by the minute. How could we even try to change the wake alone?

A far better place for our efforts is back onboard where we can begin to influence that which creates the wake. The ship's heading, its trim, the engine speed can all be adjusted in the light of both our intended destination and the conditions around us. Once all of these factors are optimised, aligned even, we will start to see the vessel behave in a new way. Slowly at first, since there are few instantaneous changes in vessels of this scale. Eventually, the vessel will be sailing in the way intended and then, but only then, can we gaze aft and see the wake that will tell of our improved progress through the seas.

There are a couple of other indicators of alignment at this corporate level. One is the principal currency of information within companies – finances. Success in reaching outcomes will usually be measured in monetary terms, either by profitability, return on capital employed, budget employed or any other specific measure. Consistent poor performance relative to industry norms might indicate some misalignment in the organisation. Performance below budget on a consistent basis represents some mismatch between aspiration and daily performance. Wherever organisations have financial measures of success, we need to look to these for evidence of the degree of alignment.

Lastly, relationships within corporations at the senior levels are a great indicator of the state of alignment. Disagreements over strategy are inevitable, indeed healthy debate often requires that we examine opposing options. Lasting disagreement is misalignment. Directors beware.

Leverage and use of the model

Aligning each of the distinctions is only part of the value of this model. There is another valuable facet to the model which we need to share here, although its importance will become obvious as you read the chapters of Part 2. This is where we discuss the real challenges businesses face at present. In each of the instances we

> **Of even greater importance than right action is right attitude.**

examine it is clear that action is needed to get the outcomes we desire. Of even greater importance than right action is right attitude.

If our purpose, identity and values are correctly aligned then the right action will come as a relatively easy matter. The alternative is to try to graft correct actions onto misaligned attitudes. This can be done, but only by great powers of concentration and conscious thought, since the process is guaranteed to fail as soon as we allow our concentration to drop.

The universal alignment model acts as a hierarchy in one important way. By making changes at the highest levels we set up the conditions where all the lower distinctions can change. For instance, the adoption of any shift in our sense of purpose will create shifts in our sense of identity and changes in the attendant values and beliefs. This can release new capabilities and behaviours or actions.

The reverse is not necessarily true. Taking action does not automatically give rise to consequent changes at the higher levels. So when looking to make changes in a system we are wise to realise that the most leverage exists with the highest distinctions. Becoming deliberate and skilful in dealing with these higher distinctions is one of the most effective ways of putting this model into operation.

- Introduction
- Feedback
- Aligning action
- Getting the leverage to realign

2

ACTION – THE VISIBLE APPLICATION OF ENERGY

- ■ **Introduction**
- ■ **Feedback**
- ■ **Aligning action**
- ■ **Getting the leverage to realign**

Introduction

Our journey through the alignment of outcomes begins with the final 'unfair' action – which we call 'ideas' along with its close associate – feedback. While what we can be absolutely sure of, any comparison organises them is that before thinking, deliberating and planning is extension, a refer to moving into an action phase will emerge. Though still a character at best.

The distinction between thought and action matters. Not at some point energy will be put into activities that have defined boundaries and tangible results. Peter Drucker, the management practice guru, once said: 'Plans are only good intentions until they deteriorate into hard work.' And the purpose of our hard work is progress – this human desire to achieve something that is more than, an improvement on, or just a difference from, what we already have? The more protracted the thinking process associated with an idea, the more the impatience for action. The realm of action is much more tangible, measurable and open for debate than its determinant – the realm of thought. This has implications for businesses, impatient for results, preferring perhaps to push for change at the action level. It is said that patience is a virtue. If the exigencies of the day keep people tethered to the grind-tone of action, then a virtuous organisation will make thinking time a priority. First, thinking smarter, then, doing better.

Performance relies upon action, and good performance needs the right action. Any type of action can be used as feedback for learning – this is how improvements are made and how performance remains on-target. While we are observing action in the wider context of performance we are also looking at the dynamics between action and feedback. We use metaphor to show the respective merits of a number of different responses to feedback. Let us take a look at performance first. Figure 2.1 suggests three components that make up performance in an organisation:

Introduction

Our journey through the alignment distinctions begins with the most familiar – action – which we will address along with its close associate – feedback. One thing of which we can be absolutely sure in any competitive organisation is that before thinking, deliberating and planning is exhausted, a sense of moving into an action phase will emerge. 'Enough talk! It's time for action!'

The distinction between thought and action ensures that at some point energy will be put into activities that have defined boundaries and tangible results. Peter Drucker, the management practice guru, once said: 'Plans are only good intentions until they deteriorate into hard work.' And the purpose of our 'hard work' is *progress* – this human desire to achieve something that is more than, an improvement on, or just a difference from, what we already have. The more protracted the thinking process associated with an idea, the more the impatience for action. The realm of action is much more tangible, measurable and open for debate than its determinant – the realm of thought. This has implications for businesses, impatient for results, preferring perhaps to push for change at the action level. It is said that patience is a virtue. If the exigencies of the day keep people tethered to the grindstone of action, then a virtuous organisation will make thinking time a priority. First, thinking smarter, then, doing better.

Performance relies upon action, and good performance needs the right action. Any type of action can be used as feedback for learning – this is how improvements are made and how performance remains on-target. While we are observing action in the wider context of performance we are also looking at the dynamics between action and feedback. We use metaphor to show the respective merits of a number of different responses to feedback. Let us take a look at performance first. Figure 2.1 suggests three components that make up performance in an organisation:

1 **Perception** – my perception of purpose, mission and role which will have a strong influence on my values and beliefs. If I perceive my role to be that of educator, I will value education as a method of work and this will provide me with a reference structure for setting future outcomes.

2 **Outcome setting** – following this example through, outcomes will be heavily influenced by the value I put on education, and the beliefs I hold that influence my role as an educator. Outcomes will provide direction for my actions.

3 **Action** – what I do as a consequence of forming perceptions, values and beliefs will be my results.

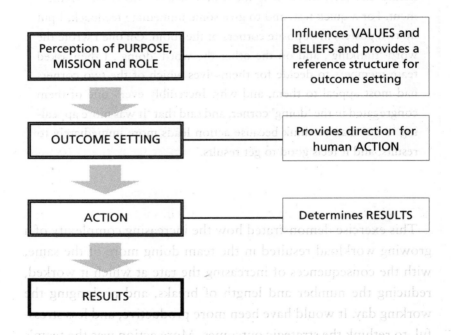

[Note: These components of performance are relevant for both macro-level (company) and micro-level (individual) performance.]

This is a simplistic way of thinking about performance, and it is simplicity which allows us to recognise how much of what is done in the name of action is a result of thinking rather than doing. With so much focus on tangible, visible actions the thinking beneath the iceberg of performance can become neglected. Here is a snapshot from a seminar we ran some years ago that provides an insight into the hurdles some teams are striving to clear in their pursuit of enhanced performance.

> I was invited to run a seminar for a management team that was suffering from having too much work of an increasingly complex nature. My brief was to help the team find a solution to its predicament. For a quick test, and to give some immediate feedback, I put up two posters in opposite corners of the room. On one I wrote the word 'thinking', and on the other the word 'doing'. I then asked team members to decide for themselves which of the two corners had most appeal to them, and why. Incredibly every one of them congregated in the 'doing' corner, and said that 'It was more appealing to act than to think because action leads more immediately to results, and it feels good to get results.'

This exercise demonstrated how the increasing complexity of a growing workload resulted in the team doing more of the same, with the consequences of increasing the rate at which it worked, reducing the number and length of breaks, and prolonging the working day. It would have been more productive, and less stressful, to rethink the strategic outcomes. More action was the team's imperative, an inadequate strategy for coping with the changing complex environment.

We are all faced with choices about how to deal with an increasingly complex world of work and business. The key question is, where is our attention focused? Is it:

- on the quality and quantity of tasks
- on being more efficient or effective at doing the task
- on what we want to achieve by doing the task
- on what doing the task actually means in the wider system of self, team, organisation and work in general?

Feedback

Feedback is the key ingredient of performance.

Without feedback any attempt to improve performance would be a stab in the dark. Feedback involves a simple loop with two dynamics:

- receiving feedback from the external environment
- responding to it.

We work from the assumption that feedback exists for everyone, but some people seem to have more flexibility in their response to it than others. It is possible to be unaware of feedback completely, in which case it is not feedback, but data. Data become feedback when we choose to acknowledge them and use them proactively for our benefit.

Feedback is very much a part of organisational life. Enormous amounts of energy and resources are invested in gathering data which are fed back into the system in the hope of improving performance. Some organisations seem to have an insatiable appetite for gathering data and measuring changes in the system. One international company we have worked with spends months each year collecting data for the purpose of succession planning, but then neglects to feed information back in any systematic way to the key individuals implicated in the data. The result is an incomplete feedback loop and some highly confused people with no better idea of the direction in which their careers might go. In our general experience we find that more effort is expended in capturing data for the purpose of control than is put to feeding back information to the people who are able to use it to improve their performance.

Another aspect of feedback which we encourage clients to explore is the difference that can be created by responding in different ways. Having the data is one thing, deciding what to do about them is another. Figure 2.2 shows the three components of performance with four possible feedback loops. These feedback loops have increasing impact on alignment which can be explained with the help of some simple metaphors.

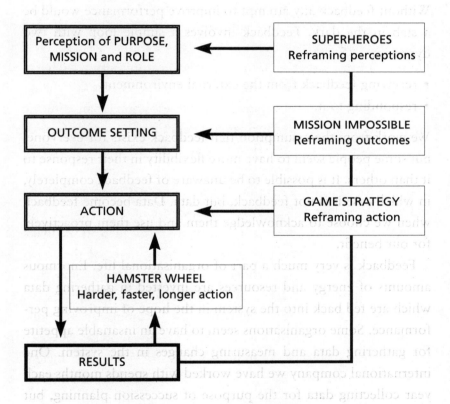

**Figure 2.2
Performance
feedback loops**

■ The hamster wheel

A hamster runs inside its wheel and gets nowhere. It runs faster and still gets nowhere. It slows down or stops and it is still in the same place. If the purpose of the wheel is to exercise, this is achieving the outcome, but I wonder what the hamster is *actually* trying to achieve?

It is possible to respond to feedback like the hamster – if feedback indicates you are not getting anywhere then work harder and faster for longer. This type of response suggests that there is little conscious learning about the situation, instead any data being fed back are quickly used to generate more action. This is OK if you live in an unchanging environment where life consists of ritual and rules, and where there is little pressure to change – all you need to do to survive is more or less of the same.

Many tribal societies function through ritual and rules handed down from ancestors generation after generation. In Papua New Guinea, for instance, the cultural rituals of communities had been, until recently, unaltered for thousands of years. That is fast changing with the arrival of logging companies from Japan offering large sums of money to tribal landowners for their timber forests. The consequence is forest destruction and a complete change to the environment with both short- and long-term adverse effects.

Being for the most part unaware of these consequences, the indigenous people of Papua New Guinea are now presented with a massive dilemma. They have habitually responded to feedback from changes to their environment by doing more of the same. This is all they have ever needed to do. But to survive today they need to respond in different ways, and that will not come easy. Through the sale of their land they are becoming grossly misaligned with their culture. What was a mainly agricultural economy is being displaced by industrial forestry. Wherever ancient and modern civilisations have emerged you are more than likely to find suffering among the ancients. The plight of Plains Indians, Aboriginals and Inuits is further proof of how indigenous peoples are being limited by their habitual responses to feedback which, up until recent times, have been adequate for survival, but which now provide insufficient for the kind of technological and social changes we are experiencing in the world.

In just one generation the indigenous people of Nuuk, Greenland, have experienced profound social transformation that has brought bingo halls, video stores, mobile phones and HIV to a land which used to support a more traditional way of life based on hunting and fishing. Incidents of suicide among young men are common. They have lost a sense of purpose in their life. Their strategies for survival as hunters and fishermen are no longer appropriate for responding to the profound changes affecting them today. Eventually, after years of struggling to stay on the hamster wheel they have been forced off by changes to the very fabric of their existence.

In business, hamster wheel responses are manifested in fire-fighting and bureaucracy. Where there is a stable unchanging environment, or where people work at 'holding things together', you can be sure to find a feedback response similar to hamster wheel. This may be a very appropriate response for a monastery, but it is unlikely to be adequate for any business with competitors, and certainly for any organisation with a focus on performance. Firefighting, holding the fort and 9–5 routines are indications of hamster wheel responses in individuals. They are likely to prefer similarity, avoiding situations presenting difference.

> In business, hamster wheel responses are manifested in firefighting and bureaucracy.

Bureaucracy, rules, strict procedures and 'job's worth syndrome' typify hamster wheel responses at team or group level putting the procedure at a higher priority than needs of customers and other groups in the organisation. Even when a procedure ceases to be useful or effective the response is to act as if it still is and persuade everyone else that they should fall in line with the procedure. In comparison to other types of response, hamster wheel uses the most energy to get the least change and the lowest quality learning.

> In comparison to other types of response, hamster wheel uses the most energy to get the least change and the lowest quality learning.

■ Game strategy

Getting out of the hamster wheel we move up to game strategy. Football team managers know all about strategy, which might consist of swapping players, learning new team tactics, formations and manoeuvres, increasing fitness and stamina and developing skills. While a great deal of energy goes into making such changes to strategy, the purpose remains the same. To score goals and win.

Game strategy is as important to a football team as business strategy is to organisations. But business strategy is more complex because there are many more variables to consider. You can work hard to improve a business strategy and yet still shoot for the wrong goal. Unlike football however, in business the goals change, and very often goals get confused with strategy. Because of the ease with which this can happen we will define strategy in the context of performance, as there are many definitions and views available from different perspectives of organisational life. To begin thinking about strategy we have an experience to share about a man and his dog.

> You can work hard to improve a business strategy and yet still shoot for the wrong goal.

Strategy often gets blurred with goals. This is another reason

We have a golden retriever named Bonnie. When Bonnie was about 9 months old we began trying to train her to dive into the river. Golden retrievers are supposed to like water. The strategy consisted of throwing a stick into the river and shouting 'fetch'. But alas, after many days of doing this, Bonnie's paws remained firmly planted on the river bank. Slightly frustrated by this we intensified the strategy by throwing bigger sticks and shouting louder and more encouragingly. But still no luck. Then came the breakthrough we were looking for. We improved the strategy by throwing chocolate biscuits instead of sticks, and applauded as Bonnie leaped through the air, splashing open-mouthed into the river. After a dozen or so dives Bonnie had coded this behaviour into an automatic response. Once a dog learns a new behaviour it can repeat it perfectly on demand any time it is given the trigger signal. The only thing that will prevent Bonnie from diving into the river after a chocolate biscuit is something threatening about the river, such as a noisy boat or an aggressive swan.

why outcomes are used to steer a course for the future, in preference to goals which put a stake in the ground. We have witnessed many strategy meetings in which the thrust of debate swings from goals to strategy and back again until there is little distinction between them. In my attempt to teach Bonnie to dive into the river, I confused the goals with the strategy. Now she will dive into the river, but only for a chocolate biscuit. The strategy became part of the goal for her. Outcomes require a different type of attention from strategy. They should be worthwhile and motivating, and they need to be well-defined. So by stripping out goals we can more easily focus on adopting courses of action that will result in outcomes being achieved, and this definition is as applicable to individuals and teams as it is to organisations.

> Outcomes require a different type of attention from strategy. They should be worthwhile and motivating, and they need to be well-defined.

Game strategy is perhaps the most common response to feedback in organisations. It has spawned the total quality movement and other management methodologies under the category of 'continuous improvement'. The western world learned a hard lesson from the Japanese about improvements to processes with their highly effective strategy for continual refinements. This approach helped them to create the market for calculators and a plethora of other electronic gadgets and devices. Here, process is a method of changing something and is usually associated with action-oriented words like training, improving, servicing, engineering, producing. Process improvement is an accepted and proven method of increasing effectiveness and efficiency.

Dallas-based Southwest Airlines wanted to achieve greater operating economies so that it could keep its fares low. It had succeeded in reducing refuelling time to 40 minutes, faster than all competitors, but driven by a desire to achieve further economies it changed the context of its thinking by benchmarking, not against its own industry as is the norm, but against a Formula 1 racing team. This switch of context allowed a breakthrough in the traditional way of thinking framed by what it thought was necessary, to set new horizons of possibility. This resulted in a further reduction to refuelling time from 40 minutes to an astonishing 12 minutes! A very effective game strategy feedback loop.

■ Mission impossible

Stepping up from game strategy we arrive at Mission Impossible, named after a TV series popular in the 1960s and 1970s, more recently the inspiration for a film of the same name. At the beginning of each episode, the secret agent would receive instructions over an audiotape set to self-destruct immediately after being played. Imagine yourself in this situation: you never know what the assignment is going to be, you have no preconceived idea of the mission or how to achieve it. Every mission is different. The strategy you would use for rescuing an abducted president would be completely different from the strategy you would use for disarming a nuclear device. The skills needed may, or may not, be similar, but the strategy is likely to be very different.

The missions stated by some organisations may seem impossible, especially with the intensity of competition in many markets, but the word 'impossible' is not a useful word in modern corporations. Outcomes set the framework for pursuing a mission, but they can also limit the possible options available by putting too tight a boundary around what must be achieved. Action without clear outcomes is like sailing a boat without a compass. Outcomes provide direction and enable individuals to make confident and appropriate decisions for the benefit of themselves and their organisation, but they must be well-formed, and have a certain degree of specificity. What is required is a flexible approach to outcome setting. Here is an example from our own consulting experience.

> **Action without clear outcomes is like sailing a boat without a compass.**

On this occasion, our brief was to investigate the reasons for poor customer service. From the heated exchanges at monthly client review meetings senior management believed that employees needed training in how to interact professionally with the client. This belief defined the goal of training the people. Our initial observation as we walked into their office was the employees' physiology – closed postures and lowered heads were clear signs of a troubled team. This was a high pressure, intense environment full of problems. No one was smiling. There were lots of creased brows with a great deal of rushing around. There were small groups of people gathered around reports, looking intense, willing the figures to improve. Voice tones were harsh and conversations rushed to economise on time, and there were frequent commands from managers to the troops: 'This has got to drastically improve', 'You'll have to better these figures, this is appalling service'.

Clearly, training was not the answer – not customer service training anyway, and not technical training. These were highly skilled computer network analysts, and they knew their stuff. The goal of 'training' was entirely inappropriate. There was something more fundamentally wrong, a massive misalignment somewhere, and on the second day we discovered what it was. Agreements between the customer and service provider defining the scope and level of service provision were non-existent. No one knew what the boundaries were to the service they were providing, and so they were often asked to do things which they were unsure of, and their physical, emotional and intellectual energy was being drained. So not only was the management's goal of training inappropriate, there was no clear agreement for service provision. This resulted in indecision, and consequently high stress, low job satisfaction and reduced commitment. It appeared that managers had not attached sufficient importance to the lack of a service agreement. The problem was perceived as behavioural and so this is the lever they chose to pull, which of course served only to worsen the situation for all concerned.

With a misdirected goal, and unclear outcomes, actions were achieving very little more than keeping people busy and stressed. Status quo was being maintained by hamster wheel feedback loops. To make progress the management team had to shift their attention to mission impossible and reframe the outcome. They had been so close to the problem, so physically connected to their current strategy, that it was difficult for them to realise a way out. They couldn't see the wood for the trees. A well-defined outcome shared by the whole team finally provided the propulsion necessary to fuel and direct people's energy. An agreement on service levels was eventually drawn up and the team soon began to improve the service it was providing.

■ Superheroes

My youngest son liked to play being superheroes. One moment he would be Spiderman, and a while later he would be the Incredible Hulk, or perhaps Superman. The change of identity would allow him to use different superpowers to destroy the enemy and save the world. He could not do it all as one character. Staying alive and saving the world was only possible by switching characters to meet the context of the particular evil created by his imagination.

I can remember when shoe shops were shoe shops – the smell of leather and walls lined with shoes of different styles, black, brown or beige. I recently walked into a Dr Marten's store and noticed how the shop resembled a modern music store with artistic displays of multicolour boots indiscriminately placed amid a decor of youth expression. The place was filled with young people socialising and buying boots. In the face of increasing competition, Dr Marten had evolved its identity by strengthening its link with youth culture and turning its stores into gathering places.

In another superheroes example, the human resources director of a large global consumer goods organisation recognised the need for HR to have a role at the top of each of its operating companies. This would ensure the ongoing provision of smart people into an expanding business, a crucial factor in a world market with an increasing shortage of experienced professionals. This director is clearly thinking in superheroes mode, responding to his perception of the environment by enabling his HR team to reframe its identity from support function to business partner. This is a very topical issue for HR chiefs and those that are striving for recognition from their top teams will best succeed by making appropriate perception and identity shifts using superheroes thinking. This feedback loop suggests a change to the perception of purpose, mission or role – a loop which more organisations are using to remain successful.

In another example, one of our clients, previously a large brewer and beer retailer, changed its identity to become a hospitality retailer spreading its activity to a series of theme pubs, leisure complexes and hotels. There are many other examples of superhero responses such as petrol stations which have become retail points for all manner of purchases, petrol being but one product.

When describing goals there is a tendency to work from evidence that exists in our immediate environment. The larger the organisation, the more evidence there is to influence what we think is necessary and what is possible. Necessity shackles possibility. This is understandable when you consider the effort required to convince other people, departments, divisions or companies to join your quest for higher order change. You may have noticed that the four feedback loops enable increasing amounts of change to what people do, and how they do it. The results are equally exponential to performance. With hamster wheel you do not change much at all except to put more effort into doing the same things. Using game strategy you reframe operational processes. With mission impossible you reframe outcomes and processes, and using superheroes you reframe perception, outcomes, and processes. The further back in the thinking process that you reframe, the more leverage you get for improving performance. If you have ever experienced a belief change by a chief executive or president you will know what 'high leverage' means in the context of alignment.

> **Necessity shackles possibility.**

Aligning action

The universal model of alignment clearly shows the type of adjustments necessary to align behind any particular purpose. In the case of a perception shift, as for the hospitality retailer, effort will be required to establish a new set of values and beliefs. Resources will also be required to ensure capability is developed, and people will find themselves performing different activities. In many cases, however, if one or more of these aspects are neglected, misalignment will ensue.

There are some common responses to misalignment in organisations. Training is one method used to attempt to align people with new attitudes and behaviours. Replacing the people is another method. Changing the business process by outsourcing or some other means is gaining in popularity. All these methods are appropriate in some contexts. What we have noticed, however, is that the intended performance improvement does not always emerge as a result of the change.

■ Signs of misaligned action

A company's espoused mission and value statements mean nothing unless they can be observed in its employees' behaviour. No one is fooled by a company's glossy brochure telling how good it is at customer service if this is not demonstrated at the customer interface. A company lives and dies by the value it can bring to its customer, and you can spot a misalignment in behaviour in a number of ways. There is no rocket science to this, we experience it every day, and we have learned to tolerate it.

> A company's espoused mission and value statements mean nothing unless they can be observed in its employees' behaviour.

We expect our organisations to be political, to have competing teams, to harbour pockets of dissatisfaction and imperfection – this has generally become accepted as the norm. But there is a difference between accepting these things without response, and using these situations as indicators to pull high leverage levers for change. What we need to do is confront these daily signs of misalignment and use them to improve performance.

Recently we were asked to help an ineffective management group. We were shown one of those travelling email messages that gets longer as each recipient takes a defensive stance and points the finger at another department. The antagonist among them was a chief accountant, who clearly wanted to get his message across regardless of the views, ideas or experiences of others in the loop. When we reported this back to the general manager who initially gave us the brief his comment was, 'That's the chief accountant for you, every so often he lifts up the tent flap and urinates in the tent to stir things up – he certainly has an effect on people.' Unfortunately, the result on the effectiveness of the team was adverse and the general manager knew this, but neither he, nor the chief accountant, seemed to have either the flexibility or the inclination to try an alternative course of action.

What I noticed was a huge incongruence between what people said about teamwork, communication and service quality, and what they could be observed doing (see Figure 2.3). In this situation, there were three options for alignment. The general manager could openly adopt the values and beliefs that 'blame and stirring up is the way we get things done around here' or he could help the team change its action to fit the values and beliefs pertaining to communication, teamwork and service quality. The third option was to change both values and action. Any of these paths will lead to alignment. The question is which change is the most useful and appropriate for this team in its work context?' Is there a clear purpose to align with?

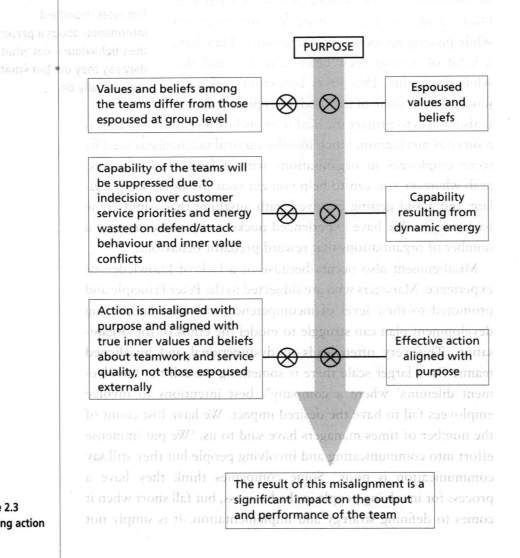

Figure 2.3
Aligning action

Chris Argyris[1] of Harvard Business School has been writing for many years about incongruence. Some people have two sets of beliefs: the professed, or espoused beliefs and those they act out in real life. Whatever people believe they believe, there is usually a fall-back position to a master behavioural response. The most important information about a person is their behaviour – not what they say they do, but what they actually do.

Tom Brown Jr. describes, in his fascinating book *The Tracker*,[2] the peculiar feeding habit of the junco bird, found in some parts of Australia. On the ground juncos are extremely jittery birds, constantly watching for predators while picking up food from the ground. They have a habit of turning their heads this way and that while doing this. This jittery behaviour causes the junco to drop some of the food it has picked up, but

> **The most important information about a person is their behaviour – not what they say they do, but what they actually do.**

it also works to protect the bird from its hostile environment. It is a survival mechanism, much like the survival mechanisms used by some employees in organisations with defend/attack cultures: grab whatever you can to help you get your job done, keep vigilant and avoid getting involved with anything that could come back on you. We have experienced pockets of junco culture in a number of organisations that reward predator behaviour.

Misalignment also occurs because of a lack of knowledge or experience. Managers who are subjected to the Peter Principle and promoted to their level of incompetence without a supporting development plan can struggle to model the ethos of the organisation. This very often leads to dysfunctional and misaligned teams. On a larger scale there is something we call the 'involvement dilemma' where a company's best intentions to involve employees fail to have the desired impact. We have lost count of the number of times managers have said to us, 'We put immense effort into communicating and involving people but they still say communication is poor.' Some companies think they have a process for involving people in the business, but fall short when it comes to defining strategy and implementation. It is simply not

> **Real involvement engages people in the entire scope of their work, including the design of strategies and processes that affect them.**

enough to send out employee surveys and respond with a plan hatched in the boardroom. Real involvement engages people in the entire scope of their work, including the design of strategies and processes that affect them.

A typical misalignment at organisational level can happen when a company decides to implement a management methodology such as TQM or empowerment.

> One large company implemented empowerment by issuing a procedure and within three months things had fallen apart because there was no support for people through the change. The consequence of this was a huge misalignment of action resulting in a training programme to teach people how to empower and how to be empowered. This was unfortunately perceived as a 'soft prescription' and had little effect other than to run up significant costs. The problem, although observable in people's actions, did not lie at the behavioural level. The very people who had decided that empowerment would be a good thing, the executive director team, had only intellectualised about it. They had not visualised it and were not living it themselves, and so were not role models of how to empower and be empowered.

This is an important point. Executive teams sometimes forget that their organisations look to them as role models for behaviour.

> **Executive teams sometimes forget that their organisations look to them as role models for behaviour.**

Dual focus and standards can dissociate executive teams from the responsibility for others' actions. The most respected and effective CEOs are those whose behaviour is congruent with the organisation's espoused ethos and who recognise their responsibility as a role model. This can only be achieved when there is a sincere belief in the values of the organisation.

Getting the leverage to align

Knowing where to make a change for the maximum leverage begins with an awareness of existing behaviours. Categorising behaviour under the four responses to feedback, and then comparing these against the alignment model will suggest where to get the maximum leverage for change. Work through the following questions to reflect on your own personal responses to your environment.

Over the past 6 months how many times have you:

- Extended your working hours in response to an increasing workload?
- Changed the way you perform a certain task?
- Redefined a goal to better suit a business outcome?
- Reframed a value to better fit a particular purpose?
- Questioned one of your own beliefs about the work you do?
- Reflected on your sense of identity attached to a particular role?

Your responses here can be viewed as a balance of your typical responses to your work environment. Are you comfortable with the way it is balanced now? If not, how would you want to address the imbalance? How can you get the most leverage to make the changes you want for yourself? Which distinctions of the alignment model will you focus on? These questions should help you to develop more of a choice in the way you respond to your environment at work.

There are few contexts in today's sophisticated technological cultures where hamster wheel responses are appropriate, yet they do exist to some degree in many organisations, and it is highly likely that where they do exist you have inertia and misalignment with one or more distinctions of the alignment model. The key principle is that:

The more change you want the higher the alignment level at which you need to be responding.

Organisations that are aligned are probably reframing at all levels on a continuing basis. The more ineffective an organisation becomes, the higher the level of response required.

Recognising the symptoms of misalignment and deciding to do something about it is the simplest stage in any move to create a different set of circumstances. Anyone pushing for difference will recognise the fundamental need to encourage people to want to think and act differently for themselves. Later in the book there is a set of principles to guide evocators of purposeful change. If you are going to respond to your environment with superhero and mission impossible levels of thinking, then you need effective communication skills for convincing others to invest their precious time and energy in your ideas. This is especially so if the misalignment is rooted in the CEO's belief system.

Notes

1 Chris Argyris (1993) *Knowledge for Action: A Guide to Overcoming Barriers to Organizational Change*. Jossey-Bass Management.
2 Tom Brown Jr. (1979) *The Tracker*. Berkeley Publishing Group.

CAPABILITY AND THE HIDDEN POTENTIAL

Introduction

A hundred years ago man's capability to fly a rocket ship to the moon, walk upon its surface and return to tell of the experience was a far-fetched idea. Today we may be equally disbelieving of our capability to travel through time, even though a number of respected scientists around the world have been working on it for many years. It seems that the more we achieve, the more we move towards an acceptance of further possibility. It may not be too difficult to imagine a more efficient public transport system powered by some as yet uninvented means of propulsion. The imagination does not have to stretch too far for this, but what about human colonisation of other planets? Too much to believe? Or just a matter of time? It seems the further away from reality we stretch our imagination the weaker our belief in possibilities.

> It seems the further away from reality we stretch our imagination the weaker our belief in possibilities.

What does this have to do with business, and with our concept of alignment? Well, if you look at the changing business environment it is not so long ago that we would have questioned the viability of supermarkets becoming banks, record companies becoming airlines, videotelephony, the internet, home computers, satellite TV and a host of other innovations that are now a way of life for an increasing number of people. Behind all new ideas are people whose perception of the possible stretches a little further than the average.

> Behind all new ideas are people whose perception of the possible stretches a little further than the average.

Distant horizons

Human progress comes about when individuals succeed in stretching their perception of the possible. It has been claimed that, given favourable genetic and environmental conditions, a new-born child has the potential capability to do and become anything. For a babe in arms the horizon of achievement may lie far away in the future, but at no other time is it as far reaching. As babies grow into young children and experience more of the world, false perceptions and limiting beliefs begin to cloud their horizons. Other people will imprint their values and beliefs upon them, often with good intentions, but drawn from their own past experience where they once had more relevance than in the present.

> For a babe in arms the horizon of achievement may lie far away in the future, but at no other time is it as far reaching.

At home they are influenced by the family system and those responsible for their well-being. At school they will be limited by their teachers' abilities and by the rules and regulations drawn up for the group rather than for the individual; and the pressure to win academic status will ensure that the label 'failure' can be used whenever standards of achievement fall short of expectations. Their peer group, while testing their strength of character, will exert pressures tending to conformity, the suppression of originality and the disparagement of high ideals. Finally, and most insidious of all, because its influence is exerted in the form of entertainment, the all-pervasive media which will occupy so much of their leisure time. The result of all these influences is a metaphorical screen obscuring or blurring their vision of the distant horizons of possibility.

We all have a different experience of reaching adulthood, fleeing the nest with our personalised screen of obscurity to make our way in an increasingly competitive world. Nature may have an influence on some people through its gifts of talent, but it is our response to the circumstances of our growing up that determines the extent of our social conditioning and subsequently our perception of our capability. In India, young elephants are put alongside mature elephants to learn the work of forest clearing. At night the young elephants are secured by a leg chain to a stake in the ground. As the elephants grow they develop the strength to pull the stake easily out of the ground, but they do not try because they have conditioned themselves into believing that they cannot do it.

Every child is born a genius. [Albert Einstein]

Learning about potential and capability has in the past been the confine of social sciences operating outside the hard-edged boundaries of business organisations. Today, potential and capability are moving into the spotlight as significant influences on organisational innovation, flexibility and progress. Capability is potential, the potential to apply experience, knowledge, skills and attitude to achieve a defined outcome. Capability has often been thought of as needing to be demonstrated behaviourally, but this is like measuring the energy in a battery only by recording what duty the battery has been on previously. Capability is more to do with future possibilities. There are many factors affecting a person's true potential, which is always far greater than anything they have ever demonstrated. If you look around in your organisation you may see potential lying dormant or suppressed; people doing tasks for which they may be unsuited or unskilled; low levels of motivation caused by cultural constraints, personal limiting beliefs or in some cases a lack of opportunity to excel in a desired area of activity. The growing challenge for business leaders today is to unleash suppressed energy and direct it toward achieving business objectives. Then people can begin to redefine the horizons of possibility for themselves, and their organisations.

> There are many factors affecting a person's true potential, which is always far greater than anything they have ever demonstrated.

> The growing challenge for business leaders today is to unleash suppressed energy and direct it toward achieving business objectives.

You may know organisations that are achieving this. It is not some state of nirvana, although it may seem like it for people in organisations where less effective people management methods prevail. A growing number of organisations are today realising the benefits of tapping into the greater potential people have to offer.

To be where we are, and to become what we are capable of becoming, is the only end in life.
[Robert Louis Stevenson]

Bill O'Brien,[1] president of Hanover Insurance from 1979, spent 25 years being driven by the premise that almost every person has an enormous reservoir of potential, both for improved performance and for happiness. When asked by Peter M Senge of MIT Sloan School of Management what was involved in organisational design O'Brien replied, 'Organisational design is widely misconstrued as moving around boxes and lines. The first task of organisation design concerns designing the governing ideas of purpose, vision, and core values by which people will live.' This was more than just fanciful talk from O'Brien who was able to demonstrate measurable increases in human performance and, as a consequence, improved financial performance for the company.

Spending just a few hours in an organisation such as Hanover is long enough to sense the abundance of dynamic energy. Harnessing this greater contribution is something which increasing numbers of enterprises are tuning into every day. Some of them may be your competitors.

Tapping into the source of energy

Anna, a young student, was sitting at a market café in Marrakesh when a man came and sat beside her. The man looked very weary and sighed as he lowered his sagging torso into the chair. 'You look like you could do with a rest,' said Anna. 'A rest? I'm on vacation this very moment, but there are too many people here for my liking. I would much rather be on a deserted beach.' A few moments later a woman came by. She was much older than the man Anna had been talking to, but she had a spring in her step and a radiant smile.

She sat down next to Anna and gestured to a waiter for his attendance. 'Good day,' she said to Anna. 'So many things to do, people to see, places to go, and it will soon be dusk.' 'Are you on vacation?' asked Anna. 'Vacation? You could say that I suppose. I retired recently and this is one of the places I have always promised myself to visit. Isn't it a wonderful place?'

There is a dynamic energy, created from an inner motivation which can be contrasted with the suppressed energy that we experience from outer sources of coercion and constraint. In the story the man had little desire to be in Marrakesh, and his energy level reflected this, unlike the older woman who was full of energy generated from the pursuit of a personal promise. Creating environments that match opportunities to needs and desires is the most effective way of avoiding the suppression of energy while nurturing dynamic energy.

> There is a dynamic energy, created from an inner motivation which can be contrasted with the suppressed energy that we experience from outer sources of coercion and constraint.

The best way to motivate people, and mobilise their inner resources, is by creating opportunities where individuals can make an inner connection with their work, often referred to as intrinsic personal value. Without it energy may be suppressed (see Figure 3.1). One of the strongest barriers to creating the right conditions for dynamic energy is the mindset that 'we know what's best for other people', and the belief that 'we know the best way of doing something'. This may be necessary in a parental role to help children in their early years become responsible members of society, but in organisations these general frames of mind, or perceptions, create systems and structures that restrain potential, leave desires unfulfilled and energy suppressed.

It is your work in life that is the ultimate seduction.
[Pablo Picasso]

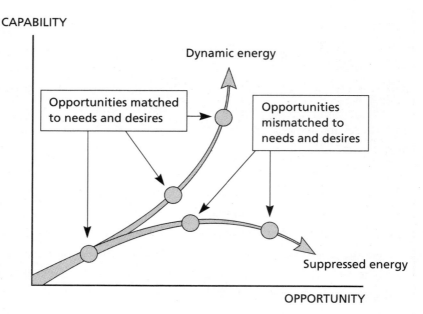

Figure 3.1
Matching
opportunities
to needs and
desire

When you look at individual situations where potential is being capped or subdued in some way, you will be sure to find a misalignment of one form or another. To examine this more closely it is important to consider the way management science has developed and how some new ideas are beginning to change things for the better.

A balancing act

Wherever groups of people come together to work there is a tendency for the paymasters to organise their environment and define rules for them. This is even more so when the work involves the use of expensive assets such as machinery, computers and skilled people. As a small company grows and develops it will need control mechanisms to help manage its different functions. Computers, with their ability to store and process information, have taken management control systems to new levels of sophistication. Schedules and projects are controlled with the aid of task and time management software; electronic clocks control attendance at the factory gate; strict and formal lines of reporting control the use of company assets; performance management systems record subjective scores on a person's contribution and there are many other such command and control mechanisms.

> The business world has emphasised intelligence of the sort that can analyse, systematise and rationalise.

Management has grown up on a diet of left-brain thinking and application.[2] The notion being that if we want to employ people we must provide them with a structured, disciplined and controlled environment otherwise they may not produce the results we want. Left-brain dominance has been responsible for the majority of developments in organisational life since before the industrial revolution. Most MBA programmes are heavily left-brain oriented. The business world has emphasised intelligence of the sort that can analyse, systematise and rationalise. Evidence shows, however, that many students are graduating with inadequate intelligence in other areas, particularly in their relationships with people, more commonly known as interpersonal skills. We do not intend to devalue left-brain thinking, rather to address an imbalance which is of concern to a growing number of successful business leaders. This is an imbalance not only of left-brain/right-brain thinking affecting creativity, but also an imbalance between intellectual and emotional intelligence affecting teamworking and the articulation of ideas. It is by balancing these aspects of organisational life that we can access the full potential people have to offer. Emotional intelligence is related to the social skills of communication, rapport building, influence, working with teams and all aspects of human interaction. It has been overshadowed by the value put on analytical ability, and only now is it becoming accepted as a prerequisite to personal effectiveness in organisations.

So, before looking at these three aspects in more detail it is worth considering the big picture of capability in an organisation. To what degree is the potential of the combined effort of the people in your organisation being limited? If you could magically align the organisation overnight what would the result be? How would you describe this in capability terms?

- In what ways would individuals be more capable?

  _____

  _____

- How would this affect the capability of teams?

  _____

  _____

- What would this difference in capability do for the organisation?

  _____

  _____

Organisational domains

Throughout our life we attend to physical, intellectual and emotional needs. Each one of us will find our own way of meeting these needs as we grow and develop. Organisations, where we spend a large part of our life, can either help or hinder the meeting of these needs, and in order to understand the connections between personal needs and the organisation we shall make reference to three metaphorical domains, the physical, the intellectual and the emotional. By understanding the effect these domains have on human effort we can begin to address the balance between physical, intellectual and emotional aspects of our environment and the balance between left-brain and right-brain utilisation. Achieving this balance will have a positive and long-term effect on how we can express our potential. The promotion of shared responsibility, enhanced communication and learning skills, more flexibility and the generation of creative ideas will all contribute to a greater capability.

The physical domain is made up of space, air quality, temperature, furniture, equipment, decor, food and drink, exercise, noise levels, odours, proximity of people and teams, clutter, tidiness, cleanliness, and, of course, behaviour. What you see, hear, touch, smell and taste define the physical domain. These aspects are very often reliable indicators of the health of an organisation. They are the direct result of behaviour, that part of human functioning which can be seen and heard, and which provides much information about the capability of a team or an organisation.

> What you see, hear, touch, smell and taste define the physical domain.

To access the emotional domain you have to delve deep down to the source of an organisation's energy. Once there, you will find that it includes bodily sensations, personal needs, ambition, desire, confidence and various other aspects of the inner self, all of which have a significant impact on energy utilisation and, therefore, capability. It is our emotions that make us human, a fact never more apparent than in our relationships with other people, and with ourselves, particularly in the competitive and complex environment of work.

> To access the emotional domain you have to delve deep down to the source of an organisation's energy.

The intellectual domain describes the applications of thinking to the design and implementation of work, the overriding influence on everything else. Let us take a closer look at each domain.

■ The physical domain

You can feel the effects of a limiting physical environment by making some changes to your own. Try blocking out the light, or turning up the heat. Put on a radio play and crank up the volume. Ask someone to interrupt you every half hour and ask you questions. Work and eat in the same place. These may seem like extreme tests of your concentration, patience and clear thinking, but many workplaces are just like this. There is a direct link between physical fitness and mental fitness. The energy we need to think comes from the physical domain. Diet, exercise, rest and relaxation determine the amount of energy we have for thinking. Working long hours with few breaks is clearly unhealthy and will lead to poor quality thinking processes.

Behaviour is an aspect of the physical environment which holds all the truths about an organisation. Not blessed with the ability to read minds or interpret emotional states, behaviour is often the only indicator of the state of any person, team or entire enterprise. Corporate mission and value statements may talk of valuing people, but the proof of the pudding is in the behaviour. It is the day-to-day interpretation of values that people respond to, not the values as written or spouted at the annual conference. In my experience managers have been quick to adopt new management fads, hoisting new slogans up the flagpole and attending conferences in the belief that people will change. In the physical domain everyone is a role model for everyone else, and managers provide the predominant role models for the organisation. If they do not change, no one else is likely to either.

> **Diet, exercise, rest and relaxation determine the amount of energy we have for thinking.**

I recall a time, some years ago, when empowerment was the flavour of the month. On one specific occasion, a senior manager returned from a one-day conference hosted by a well-renowned consultancy. The day after the conference he briefed his management team in how to empower people to make decisions for themselves, the very messages he had picked up from the conference. The managers spread the word as requested, but soon reverted to their previous prescriptive style when the quality of work dropped and customer complaints hit a new high. None of the managers had really changed. Authority had not been delegated alongside responsibility, and cynical perceptions were strengthened. Managers considered empowerment to be a method of getting an easier life, in fact this is one of the ways it had been sold to them at the conference. They hadn't understood that to empower requires a change to the relationship between themselves and the team, providing support, developing skills, working in different ways, allowing mistakes and learning from them, encouraging creative ideas, and generally facilitating the team's transition to becoming more in control of its environment.

For a relationship between two people to change for the better, both must alter their position. All too often we expect others to change to fit our own requirements. The physical domain is where you see the results of prescriptive change management.

Touring the physical domain of a fast-growing telecommunications company revealed much about its state of health. The first visit to this particular company revealed something wrong long before meeting the managing director. The decor was in a poor state and people were bunched together, in some places spilling over into each other's desk areas. Dismantled items of equipment were strewn about the place, some covered with layers of dust. Pictures on the walls were in need of a good polish. Everywhere people were in a hurry, conversations curt and body language showed signs of high stress. Rest areas were untidy, the light poor and ringing telephones were unanswered. Piles of paper, books, magazines, newspapers and other oddments created clutter. After spending some time with a number of people in this company it became clear that the intellectual domain was as disorganised as the physical. Ambiguity, lack of strategy, poor decisions, ineffective communication, and general management incompetence resulted in poor operational performance. A key consequence was a growing financial loss in an organisation where the ability to make profit was particularly highly valued.

The physical domain of a small chemical manufacturer with a mission to increase profit each year for the next five years tells a different tale. The executive offices were smart, tidy and very quiet.

The silence was unusual, reflecting the inertia throughout most of the organisation. Offices were arranged like boxes around a void of emptiness, much like the way people were managed within metaphorical boxes. This was a company whose senior managers wanted change but did little to bring it about. For some the place they currently occupy is very comfortable, and even the smallest change is just a little too scary.

The physical domain is often a consequence of the thinking done in the intellectual domain. While this is also true for the emotional domain, it is far less observable. Some years ago a North American zoo acquired two new polar bears which were to be kept in an extensive outdoor environment similar to their natural habitat. Unfortunately, work on their new home had not been completed when they arrived at the zoo, and so the bears were kept in a cage large enough to allow only three or four steps in any direction. This was their home for three months while they waited for their natural home environment to be completed. You may guess what happened. The restrictions of the cage conditioned a habitual behaviour. When the bears were eventually released into their open environment they continued to pace this way three steps, then turn and pace the other way three steps. It took a lot of hard work by the zoo staff to help the bears break out of their three-step habitual pattern, and make the most of their new environment.

The physical domain is not only an indicator of organisational health, it also has a significant influence in the opposite direction. Making improvements in our environment can definitely affect our performance and help to maximise our potential. Expect to see aesthetics, ergonomics, and even feng shui become ever more important to the architects of organised labour.

> **For some the place they currently occupy is very comfortable, and even the smallest change is just a little too scary.**

> **Expect to see aesthetics, ergonomics, and even feng shui become ever more important to the architects of organised labour.**

An audit of the physical domain

Reflect on your own organisation. Take a check of everything you can sense about the physical domain of your work, and represent your findings in no more than twelve separate words of description. Then, represent the physical domain pictorially, perhaps symbolically or as a metaphor. Try this with different groups and compare each representation. When you have done this ask yourself what your representation suggests. Ask these specific questions:

- What aspects are a result of alignments and misalignments with shared purpose, values and beliefs?

  _____

  _____

- Does the physical domain suggest any particular positive or negative aspects of the emotional and intellectual domains?

  _____

  _____

- What do you want to change?

  _____

  _____

■ The intellectual domain

This has always been the dominant domain in organisations and it continues to be so. It is learned in business schools, or simply from the corporate cultures we work in, which look for ever more effective ways of organising people and resources to achieve performance improvements. The intellectual domain encompasses all the things that can be defined as logical, rational, measurable, connected, sequential and linear in nature. The impact of the intellectual domain on capability is highly significant since it creates the boundaries of the possible and defines the necessary. It lays down the rules and builds the processes by which work gets done. The intellectual domain has developed to such a high level of sophistication, with many technological advances, that there is a real danger of overmanagement. This domain is the most written about, most diverse and most complex domain, and it holds the key to expressing capability to the full.

Since the industrial revolution technology has been taking the strain off labour and for many tasks today we only have to press a button, or turn a switch, to get the results we want. Voice activation is replacing the keyboard, and we can shop from our home computer. Soon we will have little to do physically in the work environment. Success will become more the result of how we think, not of what we do. Harnessing the power of the mind will appear as a common agenda item on corporate development programmes, and business leaders will soon be learning how to help people think more effectively. The thinking part of our brain, the neo-cortex, has been getting bigger for the past 2,000,000 years. For the last 2000 years it has been getting significantly more powerful. The full capability people have to offer organisations today can be realised by harnessing this power and engaging it in fulfilling work that has meaning for both organisations and people. In this way the intellectual domain will support maximum impact to business objectives and personal fulfilment.

> The intellectual domain encompasses all the things that can be defined as logical, rational, measurable, connected, sequential and linear in nature.

> Success will become more the result of how we think, not of what we do.

Structure and the organisation of work

Percy Barnevik, until recently CEO of Asea Brown Boveri, is recognised as a role model for leaders today. Under Barnevik's leadership the company restructured to become 1000 separate companies with 5000 profit centres and a headoffice team of a mere 200. It is a truly global company with the flexibility to operate according to local market conditions. This case shows what can be achieved when the thinking power of business leaders is focused on creating environments that naturally get the best out of people. It will be interesting to observe how Goran Lindahl, Barnevik's successor, will achieve his desire to 'give free reign to innovation, and harness the tons of human brains among the group's 216,000 employees!' It takes men of great courage and wisdom to create visions such as this.

Ricardo Semler, maverick of organisational structure, transformed the conventional hierarchy of his father's ailing company in Brazil into an effective new structure based upon giving full autonomy, responsibility and authority to people who need it. He removed the need for managers and offered skilled workers the means to set up their own business and supply him with component parts. The result of this innovative change took the company to a profitable and more secure existence. Semler created an environment allowing people to contribute fully to the running of the business.

On a recent change programme a manager responsible for publishing a range of catalogues explained about his scenario back at work. There are four teams, each performing a different function. Most of the time things went smoothly, but now and again major problems would occur and the teams would blame one another. The workflow had been designed by a project manager and each team had been told what was expected. As no one had bought into this workflow they were very quick to point a finger at its weaknesses when things went wrong. Each team felt its own contribution met requirements and so fault must lie with one of the other teams.

Situations like this happen when managers design work systems for other people and fail to recognise the importance of involving people in problem solving, creativity and decision making. It may take some courage to let go and trust people to do the right thing, but involving people at every stage of the business will pay off in the long term. Everyone thinks they have the best idea, but only a team can design the one idea that they will make work. Experts should advise, not prescribe; enable not push; support not suppress.

> **Everyone thinks they have the best idea, but only a team can design the one idea that they will make work.**

Systems

This part of the intellectual domain is proliferating at an unprecedented rate as computer technology finds more applications in the
jungle of business systems. There is a danger that systems can sti-
fle capability rather than act as an enabling tool. Systems are good
at handling complexity and taking over mundane tasks. Systems
which free people from the complexity and
drudgery of work will help to enhance overall capability of the workforce. It is quite possible, however, for systems to shackle people to technology.
The growth of call centres demonstrates this point
very well, with their echoes of the sweatshops of
the Victorian era. The idea of taking decision making away from
a person, and programming it into a computer to reduce the
potential for error, can be misguided. In one sense, it is a very
rational argument, yet the call centre industry is working hard to
find new ways of putting people and computers together in a way
that gives people more meaning in their work. Currently this
booming sector is responsible for rising levels of stress, headaches,
sickness and absenteeism at above normal levels. Staff turnover as
high as 50 percent is common in this line of work.

> **Systems which free people from the complexity and drudgery of work will help to enhance overall capability of the workforce.**

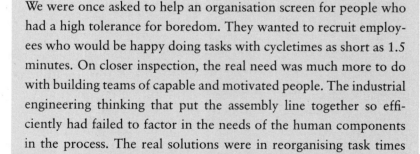

We were once asked to help an organisation screen for people who
had a high tolerance for boredom. They wanted to recruit employees who would be happy doing tasks with cycletimes as short as 1.5
minutes. On closer inspection, the real need was much more to do
with building teams of capable and motivated people. The industrial
engineering thinking that put the assembly line together so efficiently had failed to factor in the needs of the human components
in the process. The real solutions were in reorganising task times
and communication routes so the work would be more fulfilling,
not in filtering out 'unsuitable' people.

The intellectual domain is undoubtably important – business will continue to need and attract highly developed intellect to organise it in all of its complexity. Yet all too often, striving for optimal solutions blinds managers to the breadth of influences upon capability. We must remember that our work involves and revolves around people, and the human brain is still by far the biggest source of untapped potential in the universe as we know it. Let us not lose sight of this important fact, and recognise it. The source of energy for this marvellous computer we call the brain lies within us, rooted, and fired up in the emotional domain.

> The source of energy for this marvellous computer we call the brain lies within us, rooted, and fired up in the emotional domain.

An audit of the intellectual domain

Consider your own organisation and focus on the ways in which people apply their minds to the day-to-day problems which occur. Are intellect and logic highly valued? How are decisions made? What is the degree of consultation? How often are emotional consequences considered?

- What aspects are helpful to the organisation maximising its capability and pursuing its purpose?

  _____

  _____

  _____

- What aspects are a hindrance?

  _____

  _____

  _____

- What would you like to change?

  _____

  _____

  _____

■ The emotional domain

The increasing interest in emotional intelligence (or emotional quotient, EQ) is a result of the realisation that to succeed in business today you need more than professional qualifications and technical expertise. Interpersonal and intrapersonal skill is very much in demand, often as a priority over technical ability. The latter can be easily learned, whereas communication skills and social skills are thought of as difficult to acquire. You either have them or you do not. This, of course, is not true, but it does take a great deal more effort and commitment to develop social skills compared to developing skills required for most technical and professional disciplines.

> **The emotional domain must be defined by leaders.**

The emotional domain is becoming more of a priority for organisations as it holds the key to sustaining a competitive lead. Other companies may copy your structure, process, product design, strategy and all aspects of the intellectual domain, but the capability of your people is difficult to plagiarise. Of course, it can be stolen, coaxed or headhunted by those unaware of the importance of organisational alignment for stimulating wide-spread and far-reaching capability. Creative thinking and innovative ideas are vital ingredients for long-term success, and the emotional domain is where these natural human attributes can be stimulated, nurtured and developed.

The emotional domain must be defined by leaders. It is leaders who provide the role models for the type of relationships, at the core of the emotional domain, that will influence capability and performance in positive ways. No better example could be found than Julian Richer, owner of Richer Sounds who has a reputation as a Mr Motivator because of his business philosophy towards his staff. His model is simple: make sure your staff are happy and they will give good customer service which will lead to increased turnover, reduced complaints, less theft and fewer occurrences of absenteeism. Because of his success with this philosophy he is sought after by large organisations to help them do the same.

Relationships

The fact that large corporates are seeking the help of Julian Richer is a reflection on the degree of difficulty experienced by sophisticated management in their search for better relationships between management and staff. Their motivation is clearly one of improving capability and performance. Yet even with the best organised intellectual and physical domains breakdowns occur in relationships, and for a number of reasons. People fulfil roles performing certain functions and tasks. Perceptions are set, goals are described and put into action, and feedback is gathered to ascertain progress and determine next steps. These are all aspects of the intellectual domain. The moments where progress is made are in the interactions between humans, a function of the emotional domain.

> The moments where progress is made are in the interactions between humans, a function of the emotional domain.

Organisations provide us with nourishment and we each take what we need. Some people set themselves very high targets of achievement, others get more satisfaction from belonging to a team, and some people thrive on building a personal power base. David McClelland and David Burnham[3] of Harvard Business School suggest that people are motivated to seek power, affiliation or achievement. Their studies with managers show clear differences in how these three needs determine management and communication style. When these styles come together in the emotional domain anything can happen. Mismatches in communication styles can make interaction uncomfortable, or at worst intolerable. A neglected emotional domain can fester personality conflicts which are very damaging to the organisation and the people, regardless of the sophistication in structure, system, process and strategy.

Recognising the emotional domain

One of the roles of leaders in organisations is to ensure the growth of capability. At least, this is true for organisations which are themselves growing, or which are demanding more from their people. To do this requires that we create the circumstances in which it is acceptable to experience and express emotions and feelings. If we do not do this, we have a situation where individuals are stifled emotionally and the expression of capability is restricted.

> **Harvey Jackins postulates that being able to experience emotion fully and without interruption is essential to the full functioning of our human intelligence.**

As human beings we all experience emotions. Indeed, emotions have an important function to perform. Emotions arise as we digest and internalise our experience of the world around us. They are the reactions that accompany each new interaction or each new learning that we gain. Harvey Jackins, in his book *The Human Side of Human Beings*,[4] postulates that being able to experience emotion fully and without interruption is essential to the full functioning of our human intelligence. He goes on to observe that the extent to which we are unable to express the emotions that we feel is the extent to which we continue to inhabit our own private world of conditioning, with its limited horizons of capability.

Different societies have different cultural rules concerning the expression of emotion; similarly, different organisations have different thresholds beyond which the expression of emotion is unacceptable. On the one hand, we have worked in companies where a simple handshake is perceived to be overfriendly and unnecessary, and,

> **The emotional domain drives the capability of the organisation.**

on the other hand, we have colleagues from the theatre where the norm involves far more acceptance of, and display of emotion. Typical British organisations are relatively cold and unforgiving of those who seem unable to 'control' themselves. Little do they know the way in which this inhibits the capability of their people.

The emotional domain drives the capability of the organisation. It cannot sensibly be ignored, and it deserves to be stimulated, encouraged, accepted and protected.

An audit of the emotional domain

Consider your own organisation and focus on the ways in which people connect emotionally to their work. Do people show their emotions freely? How much suppressed energy is generated from negative feelings about work? How much dynamic energy is generated from positive feelings about work?

• What aspects are helpful to the organisation maximising its capability and pursuing its purpose?

_____

_____

• What aspects are a hindrance?

_____

_____

• What would you like to change?

_____

_____

The relationship between the three domains

This metaphorical approach to thinking about capability generates a dialogue about emotion and feelings not often used in intellectually dominated organisations. And the physical environment receives a higher importance than may have previously been awarded. It is the relationship between each domain which provides the understanding necessary to release more and more potential in those working within the organisation. The emotional domain is the seat of all energy, under the direct control of each individual. It is personal choice that decides where and how energy is invested. In coercive conditions people will put some of their energy into tasks as directed, but much of it will be suppressed or withheld. Tapping into the collective energy of a workforce requires an awareness, and a commitment to creating an

**Strength doesn't come from physical capacity. It comes from indomitable will.
[Mahatma Gandhi]**

environment enabling people to work towards fulfilling their needs and desires. The thinking necessary to create this is a function which takes place in the intellectual domain (see Figure 3.2).

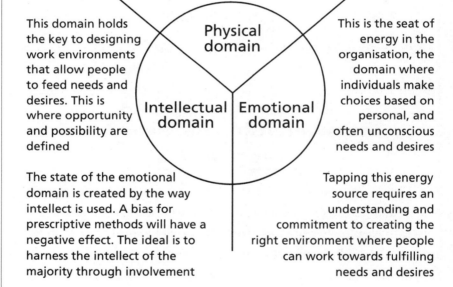

Behaviour is a manifestation of the true values, beliefs and identity of individuals. This domain provides cues to the degree of emotional connectedness with work – but only where leaders are tuning in to it

What you find in the physical domain is a reflection of the state of balance between the intellectual and emotional domains

This domain holds the key to designing work environments that allow people to feed needs and desires. This is where opportunity and possibility are defined

Physical domain

This is the seat of energy in the organisation, the domain where individuals make choices based on personal, and often unconscious needs and desires

Intellectual domain

Emotional domain

The state of the emotional domain is created by the way intellect is used. A bias for prescriptive methods will have a negative effect. The ideal is to harness the intellect of the majority through involvement

Tapping this energy source requires an understanding and commitment to creating the right environment where people can work towards fulfilling needs and desires

Figure 3.2 Relationship between the three domains

The interconnectedness of the three domains is thus highlighted. Perhaps this is no surprise, yet all too often it receives little or no conscious attention in organisations. We believe there is a great gain to be made by the careful consideration of how best to stimulate each of the domains.

We believe that the following principles apply:

- A weakness in any one of the domains will lower the overall capability which can be expressed by the system, whether that is a person or a company.
- The expression of full potential requires that each domain is, in itself, healthy and strong.
- The condition of the physical domain is an indicator of the condition of the other two domains.
- A limited ability for people to express themselves in the emotional domain will reduce their ability to perform in the intellectual domain.

Conclusion

What we have suggested in this chapter may seem like a magical formula for unleashing potential and allowing people to fulfil their true capability for the benefit of themselves and the organisation. The formula does work, we have witnessed its implementation in different ways in a number of organisations. What we have done is to draw upon our observations and experiences to create a conceptual framework.

This understanding of how the three domains interact will allow any business to create dynamic energy in the workforce. If these three levers can each be adjusted deliberately we raise the possibility of adjusting the capability of the system to be in alignment with purpose, identity, values, beliefs, action and outcomes. For companies this raises the proportion of the payroll which is being put into use. For teams it means more can be done by the same number of people combining their potentials. And for individuals it gives us some clues about the personal development which can help us to achieve our goals with the greatest ease and the least stress.

Notes

1 Peter Senge, Art Kleiner, Charlotte Roberts, Richard Ross and Bryan Smith (1994) *The Fifth Discipline Fieldbook*. Nicholas Brealey Publishing.
2 Ned Herman (1994) *The Creative Brain*. Brain Books.
3 David C McClelland and David H Burnham (1994) 'Power is the great motivator', *Harvard Business Review*, reprint 95108.
4 Harvey Jackins (1965) *The Human Side of Human Beings*. Rational Island Publishers.

4

ATTITUDES

Introduction

Imagine for a moment that we have decided to go fishing out on the lake, our clear purpose being to catch some fish. We hop aboard the boat with our rods, tackle and bait and set off. In order that we can enjoy the sport and each other's company from the outset we decided to put the boat's automatic steering on the particular heading that will take us directly into the part of the lake where we have fished successfully before.

Although the company is great the sport is less good, in fact after an hour we have caught nothing. However, we spot other fishing boats congregating at a spot on the other side of the lake and so I go up to the wheelhouse and grab the steering wheel, overriding the automatic pilot and turn the boat onto the heading that will take us over to where the fish are biting. Before long you are shouting up to me that we have found fish, they are taking the bait and you have caught a couple already. In my excitement to join in I run down and pick up my rod and soon I, too, have landed some fish and we are enjoying our success. But what happens next?

Pretty soon the nibbles dry up, there are no more fish to be taken, we seem to have lost the shoal that we had found. With no one at the wheel the automatic pilot had taken over and the boat had returned to the original heading that we set on leaving harbour. Without our conscious involvement, and outside our awareness, we have slipped back onto a setting that does not get us the results we want.

Our own progress and our own individual results can be just like that of the boat. We can manually steer by paying conscious attention to what we are doing, to our reactions and responses, to our thoughts and preferences, by taking only decisions which we have carefully considered. But, if for one moment, we take our hands off the wheel then our own autopilot takes over. And the autopilot is our attitudes which direct our behaviour when we do not put conscious attention on our thought processes – they dictate our preferences for conscious thought too.

What are attitudes?

Attitudes are a composite of our values and beliefs, the rules that we decide we will apply to our lives and our sense of identity. They are the way we have learned to think. Attitudes are a collection of thinking patterns that, together, help us to decide our responses to the complex world around us. So instead of puzzling every new situation out from first principles we can approximate the new situation to an older one for which we have learned a response. This massively reduces the difficulty of dealing with the world. We need only master a small repertoire of responses rather than be constantly fathoming out new situations.

> Attitudes are a composite of our values and beliefs, the rules that we decide we will apply to our lives and our sense of identity.

> Attitudes are a collection of thinking patterns that, together, help us to decide our responses to the complex world around us.

Recently I was thrown into jail! Fortunately only in the playful environment of a kids' adventure park which had a jailhouse for dads. My kids took great delight in putting me into the small jail, slamming the doors, ramming home the bolts and laughing at my discomfort. My one hope was a small sign on the outside which said: 'If dads are clever they can escape'. I now began to explore the jail looking for some way of getting out. Was the roof fixed on, would the bars on the windows pull out, was there a trap door or secret tunnel? Eventually, and only with someone else's help, did I find the answer. One of the doors was designed to look from the inside as if it hinged on the right but actually it hinged on the left. So, in fact, the door was open to the push all along, but so conditioned was I to 'how doors work' that I had only tried to push the door in the way it appeared to open. We are sometimes, quite literally, imprisoned by the paucity or inflexibility of our responses to the world.

In another example we might consider the archetypal Briton abroad. We do not enjoy a strong linguistic tradition in this country and most foreign people dealing with the British accept the need to speak English. Right or wrong, this leads to the situation like the tourist venturing a few words of French to one of the locals, when in search for the Post Office:

'Ou est la poste?', asks our friend, in a less than perfect French accent.

The Frenchman shrugs, willing to help, perhaps, but unable to understand.

'Ou est la poste?', gets repeated, a little slower and a little louder. Still no understanding and once again the volume goes up.

'Ou est la poste?'.

This cycle can be repeated as many times as patience and social convention allow; there is no likely solution in sight. The repertoire of response is too small to allow any other options to be tried.

A colleague was in a taxi in Tokyo, surprisingly, on his own. Our employer at that time didn't usually leave Brits alone in Japan because, with directions only in Japanese characters and very few simple ways to communicate with local people, it is easy to get lost. Chris, however, found himself in those awkward circumstances. Returning from an evening meeting, he was sitting in the back of a taxi, with no words of Japanese and a driver who didn't understand his request to go to the well-known 'Palace Hotel'. After one or two trips around this cycle of non-comprehension, it occurred to Chris to extend his repertoire, to venture into new territory. He had heard that some Japanese understood English if pronounced in Japanese fashion. Asking now for 'Parraco Hoterro', he was met by a smile that beamed comprehension at him and was rapidly transported to his destination.

Chris's attitude served him well in finding a means to communicate. Every day we are surrounded by examples where attitudes serve people well. At work, for instance, we sometimes encounter people with really helpful attitudes. What a pleasure it is to discover a service provider whose natural response, almost instinctual it seems, is to help. This person will be on the lookout for ways to assist, giving suggestions or time to the task in hand. This is an attitude which is aligned with the purpose of service.

Have you ever found the converse, someone whose attitude is at odds with this purpose? I would wager that we could all recount tales of poor service. In many of these cases the cause of the problem will not be a lack of knowledge about what to do, more often the root cause is the desire, or rather the lack of desire, to be of help.

Where attitudes are aligned with purpose they drive behaviour to find appropriate responses.

Now, we might ask these people to do something different, to be more helpful or to show initiative, to provide some service activity perhaps. Our focus with these suggestions is at the level of behaviour – will you do something different. But the problem exists at the level of attitude.

Where attitudes are aligned with purpose they drive behaviour to find appropriate responses. Where misaligned, no amount of training at the level of behaviour can overcome this completely and permanently.

How do our attitudes form, where do they come from? Let us consider attitudes as a predisposition to act in particular ways. In our attitudes, we are replaying all of the lessons that we have learned from our experience of life. Bitten by a dog at a young age, I translate this traumatic and painful experience into a belief that all dogs are dangerous, and I am going to act as if this were true. A simple enough example and one which most of us will find completely credible.

Human beings can alter their lives by altering their attitudes of mind. [William James]

What about the parallel: people who have been used to being told what to do at work, whose ideas have been discouraged and whose efforts have been channelled into never-changing routines. This way of working, enforced over a number of years, can easily be translated into its own lessons; it is not worth venturing new ideas here, whatever you think the task remains the same, repeatability is prized. Add these lessons together and we have a worker with attitudes which are unlikely to find favour with managers looking for initiative and imagination. Who is at fault?

Before we discuss the components of attitude in detail we might mention one further important point. Attitudes are contextual, they only operate in certain contexts. In different contexts, people exhibit different collections of attitudes. Large organisations are constantly surprised to learn what their employees do in their spare time. Ford Motor Company in the UK was horrified to find that the assembly workers included people able to take on high levels of responsibility in local communities, councils or the reserve armed forces. None of this capability was on show at work, and the attitudes involved at work and leisure were very different too.

> Attitudes are contextual, they only operate in certain contexts.

We are going to examine the components of attitude on an individual basis before we look at the organisational equivalent of attitude – culture.

Beliefs

Let us go back to that dog. If I have been conditioned from a young age to believe that dogs are dangerous, it is likely that I will act as if that were true in any situation. So powerful is this belief in my thinking that I will even, unconsciously, filter the sensory data available through sight, sound, smell, taste and touch in such a way to reinforce that view. I will see the long white teeth of next door's pet dog very clearly and interpret the barking I hear as a threatening noise regardless of the reason or message behind it. At the same time I will completely fail to notice how calm my neighbour is in the proximity of such a 'dangerous beast'. I am filtering the data available to me and keeping intact my view that dogs are dangerous. Robert B Cialdini in his respected study of human behaviour notes the drive to remain consistent with the stand we have taken on any issue.[1] Deep down it appears we wish to remain consistent with our own thinking and our own previous behaviour. It is hugely inconsistent with my past fears and my history of avoidance action for me suddenly to become friendly with Rex next door.

Not only does this belief influence how I see the world, it also affects how I behave in the world. I will behave consistently with this belief, crossing the road to avoid unleashed dogs, and choosing to remain on guard when in the same room as other people's dogs. Once I have adopted the belief, I will interpret the world and behave in the world as if this were true at all times, thereby demonstrating complete consistency in all aspects of my behaviour. The power of beliefs confirms one aspect of the alignment model. Beliefs clearly have the power to drive behaviour.

Beliefs clearly have the power to drive behaviour.

■ Beliefs as rules

Another way of considering the influence of our beliefs on our activities is to note the rules that govern our behaviour. Beliefs act as the unwritten rules, the codes of conduct or operating standards that help us decide what to do. Most of these thoughts have probably never even been articulated, yet we use them day after day as we meet moments of choice. Then, instead of needing to evaluate the situation afresh, from first principles, we can fall back on some underlying principles which will help us ensure our response is consistent with our broader thinking.

Beliefs act as the unwritten rules, the codes of conduct or operating standards that help us decide what to do.

I worked with a manager who wanted to exhibit even more leadership, or wanted perhaps that his leadership was recognised by more senior management in the company. In the process of reviewing Gordon's thinking patterns we found out a rule that he used to sort people in his mind. Every time Gordon met someone new she was quickly assessed in his own silent process. Those people, very few in number, who Gordon reckoned were his equal were categorised as 'OK', everyone else went into the 'dim' box. OK was a hard accolade to win, it required evidence of a quick mind and a certain amount of similarity to Gordon himself in communication style. Gordon believed that there were a lot of dim people about, and Gordon's rule was that everyone who wasn't OK was dim. That was it, inescapable, immutable: they were dim.

We need to watch what we believe, as Cardinal Newman observed in the nineteenth century. 'We can believe what we choose. We are answerable for what we choose to believe.'

■ Where do beliefs come from?

If beliefs have this leverage in both our conscious and unconscious thinking it is worth a moment to explore how they arise. We talked earlier about how people become conditioned to believe certain things. What does this mean? To understand this we need think about three principal factors:

> 'We can believe what we choose. We are answerable for what we choose to believe.'
> [Cardinal Newman]

- emotional intensity
- repetition
- authority figures.

Beliefs can be instilled into people by any of these three factors. Consider, for example, how many times a small child would need to be bitten by a dog to be convinced that dogs are dangerous. The answer will be a small number, probably one if the pain and terror of the experience are high. Anything that causes large amounts of emotion, particularly unpleasant emotion, will trigger survival reactions in us. And we quickly generalise from the singular instance to the wider belief, such as the universal truth that 'all dogs are dangerous'.

Repetition leads us to beliefs of the same degree of immutability, albeit over a longer period. For many of us, the experience of teachers as people who told us what we had done wrong was an intrinsic part of our education. The beliefs we learned from this continual criticism of the work we exposed to their view are likely to remain in some form or other. 'I'm bound to have got something wrong', or a variant of this, is a common belief we find limiting the very able adults whom we encounter in our professional development work.

Teachers need to take care for another reason. They, second only to parents, are the authority figures that we so readily 'believe' when we are young. People we admire, respect or are simply told are important, inhabit a vantage point from which they can easily influence what we understand to be right or wrong. For much of my childhood, I assumed that there was something unpleasant about people who drove company cars, such was the disgust my father had for them. And I am indebted to my Latin teacher who, when I was thirteen, told us not to believe everything we read in newspapers. 'Newspapers can be wrong,' he said, following this with the even more significant, 'Even I can be wrong sometimes!' Thank you, Mr Benson, for that invaluable lesson. My ability to sort and discriminate between pieces of information is in part based upon my belief that this is a worthwhile activity in a world where we cannot rely on everything people tell us.

Man is what he believes.
[Anton Chekhov]

■ How useful are beliefs?

For the purposes of this book we need to assess beliefs only by their likely impact on our performance. Thus we have beliefs which can be either aligned or misaligned with one or more of the other distinctions in the universal alignment model. How would we differentiate between the two? In either case, the first step is to be aware of the belief in the first place. Many of our beliefs are shy creatures, influencing our thinking unconsciously, without ever coming out into the daylight. Beliefs can be tempted out in reply to the question, 'What do I believe to be true?' Whether asking what is true about ourselves, about the world we live in or about any other specific subject, the answer will be a belief. Some answers may be facts. The sun will always rise, for example, is both fact and belief. If you remain unsure as to whether your response is a belief or a fact, qualify it with a further distinction by asking, 'What sensory-based evidence is there to determine whether or not this belief is grounded in reality?' Some things you know are objectively true, others are believed to be true but could never be objectively demonstrated to be so.

In order to begin to recognise the influence of your own beliefs reflect on your answers to these two questions:

1   What rules do you believe apply to human conduct? For example, some people believe in karma, the sense that your actions will be reflected back to you by the actions of others.

_____

_____

2   What rules of life do you believe are true for you?

_____

_____

Values

Quite simply, values are the things that we hold to be important. They share some of the attributes of beliefs, in that their influence over our thinking and our behaviour is profound, yet they operate in part without our conscious thought. We can find whole decisions and

> Quite simply, values are the things that we hold to be important.

important changes are made in our lives in accordance with our values without consciously knowing what these values are. Values are those things that we are willing to expend resources of time or energy in order to have, or to avoid. They can be attractions or repulsions, in either category they are a primary motivating factor in all of our behaviour. This is one of the ways in which they govern our performance. The other is through their role as evaluation criteria, against which we judge our own actions as good or bad, right or wrong. Our values are the internal benchmark against which all that we do can be judged.

> Values are those things that we are willing to expend resources of time or energy in order to have, or to avoid.

Once tempted out into the open we would be likely to see that our most highly placed values are abstract ideals: health, integrity or love rather than specific objects or activities. As such, they have a degree of abstraction and a breadth of meaning to us, rather than a very specific interpretation. A value such as success might have a variety of related concepts clustered together in our thinking. Given what we have said about the unconscious nature of our values, there is much understanding to be gained by the relatively simple process of articulation, the first step toward the deliberate use of values.

One of the important distinctions to make about values is the difference between ends values and means values. Success, truth or health might be the ends toward which we are working. Declared values such as money or family might be considered to be the important means by which we might realise ends values. There can be a considerable difference between valuing money, in and of itself a commodity, and placing value upon feeling

> Some beliefs seem to serve the function of rules, telling us how to interpret values through our actions.

prosperous, defined as broadly as you wish. The difference is important in many ways, but let us consider just one as an example. It may well be possible to feel prosperous with a relatively small amount of money, while an extremely rich person valuing money might yet feel unsatisfied. Which seems preferable to you?

There is also a link to be made between values and beliefs. We can perhaps imagine a particular value having several beliefs attached to it, as there are several leaves attached to any one branch of a tree. Some beliefs seem to serve the function of rules, telling us how to interpret values through our actions. Think for a moment about the value of integrity. We might not be too sure what is meant when someone tells us that this is a key value of theirs. But we would be able to recognise the beliefs attached to it. 'People shouldn't tell lies', 'It's wrong to take what isn't mine' or 'Expenses need to be completely accurate and accountable', would all be examples of beliefs, or rules if you like, that help us to live out our value of integrity.

We can talk about beliefs and values being the product of events in our formative years. It might perhaps be more accurate to say that it is our *perception* of those experiences and events which causes us to begin to interpret the world in preferred ways. Anthony Robbins tells the story of two men, the sons of a bitter, cruel father.[3] The father's life followed a downward spiral of alcohol, addiction and abuse until eventually he was jailed for murder. One of the sons turned out just like his father, repeating his behaviours in a life of crime trying to support his drug addiction, and eventually himself jailed for an attempted murder. The other man became a totally different person, a loving father and supportive husband, successful in his career and seemingly happy in his life. He values his good health and avoids drugs of any kind. Both men, when asked why their lives had turned out this way, said, 'What else could I have become growing up with a father like that?'

In the process of identifying values we will look at two important sub-sets of the family of values: towards and away from. Towards values are those things that you want more of in your life. Away from values are the things you want less of. Think about your own values for a moment, and record them here.

List the things you want more of and the things you want less of in your life, remembering that values are contextual, so be clear which context you are choosing for your answers, is it work, or home or something else.

- Away from values:

  _____

  _____

  _____

- Towards values:

  _____

  _____

  _____

Our motivation in all of the responses and decisions of daily life is provided by these values and our ability to achieve or avoid them. Unbeknown to our conscious minds, there are also rules wired into our thinking regarding how we can bring this about. These are the standards that need to be met or the conditions that need to be satisfied in order for us to judge ourselves successful.

Judith definitely wants to be good at her job, she is motivated by the success that she can achieve and the feeling of worth that she associates with her particular role within the organisation where she works. She values success but has, unfortunately, set herself criteria for feeling successful which are well-nigh impossible to meet. The product of her early life experiences is a set of extremely high standards. The result is that Judith can always see where her work could have been better, and her rule for being successful, that her work is faultless, is very seldom met. As a result she sees 'failure' even when her work is of a high standard and she feels bad. Her self-esteem scarcely has an opportunity to develop because she is constantly doing work that is not faultless, so by her own rules she has been unsuccessful.

Identity

The final aspect of attitude to discuss is identity. Identity is a label to which we attach a particular collection of values and beliefs. So, in one particular identity, we are ready with a set of responses to the world around us, in another identity we can respond and act differently.

I remember my first days at secondary school, the distinguished King Edward's School in Birmingham. I entered into a whole new environment, imposing buildings, acres of playing fields, lists of head boys and team captains gold-lettered on the wall, a library that smelled of polished wood and books. To me, newly arrived, uncertain and not knowing anyone else at the school, the sixth form boys were like giants, the first XV rugby players were gods. In contrast, I was a new bug, a particular identity most of us have experienced at some time. I took on the appropriate behaviour, somewhat quiet and shy, acting out the junior role in the dinner hall, the tuck shop or the playground.

In this school, the house system was a good mechanism for bringing boys in all years into contact with each other. Pretty soon I was acquainted with one of my heroes, the school full back, soon to be capped for England at schoolboy level. Better was to follow. Ian was not at all above talking to a mere first year and we became reasonably friendly. I can recall quite vividly how his interest in our under-12 rugby allowed me to adopt a new identity. I recognised a link between him and me – we were both representing the school, as I became a school sportsman, albeit of more modest ability and at a more junior level. Along with this new identity came a new feeling of confidence and worth in this strange new world. I was able to walk more confidently along the corridors, join in playground football with the second years or hang about near the fives courts with the older boys. I now was a part of the school, no longer just a new bug.

This process whereby we attach an agglomeration of values, beliefs and rules to an identity is largely an unconscious one, driven by our experience, unless, of course, we choose to make it deliberate. When a close colleague of mine was exploring his options to break out of a current role as a training manager into the world of consulting, he recognised his experience was limited in one crucial way. Most small consultancies require their consultants to be able to generate work, in other words to sell. But he had no significant experience of selling and knew this was to his detriment. To fill this gap he built for himself an identity as a salesman. He read, studied, observed and modelled the ways successful salespeople thought, how they acted, what they did and did not do. As a result, he felt much more comfortable with this new identity, and when required he could be a salesman and have at least a good start towards knowing how to sell.

Identity is close to the heart of who we are, our human essence, and we guard it vehemently. We hold onto our identities with our beliefs and values, regardless of how we feel about who we are. People with low self-esteem spend much of their time reinforcing their feelings about themselves, regardless of others' efforts to bring them out of their shells, which often results in further retreat.

When we talk about the past as if it were the present we are doing the same thing. Consider the unconscious intention behind this seemingly harmless statement of the type we hear people say every day: 'When I go to town I always end up spending more than I can afford.' This is a typical example of bringing past experience into the present, which unconsciously influences the future, and keeps an identity of 'over-spender' intact. The behaviour of such a person could conceivably be changed by adopting the identity of being 'moneywise'. The language would change to: 'In the past, when I have gone into town, I have spent more than I could afford. But I am learning to be smarter with my money and so today I will limit myself to spending within my set budget.'

Changing our sense of identity means thinking about our capability in different ways, breaking out of habitual mindsets and learning new patterns of thinking and behaving. Some people have great difficulty acquiring the qualities of effective managers, leaders, communicators, presenters and similar roles because they hold onto their existing sense of identity. Along with that come beliefs and values which create a barrier to learning, and more significantly, a barrier to *becoming*. In our many years of training people in organisations we have experienced some who are superb intellectual learners, but who do not have the ability to transfer their learning into action. Needless to say, we have now developed quite sophisticated models of development that help people to internalise learning and become excellent at the roles to which they aspire. Learning is often unrelated to changing identity, but this is exactly what happens. Can you honestly say that you are the same person you were five years ago? How about two years ago? What about three months ago? In what ways has your identity changed over time? Think back over the course of your adult life and reflect upon how your identity has changed.

Carpenters bend wood; fletchers bend arrows; wise men fashion themselves. [Buddha]

- Use words such as sportsman, communicator, salesman, chancer, etc. to describe your identity as a young adult:

  _____

  _____

  _____

  _____

  _____

- What significant changes have you consciously, or unconsciously made to your overall sense of identity over the years?

  _____

  _____

  _____

  _____

Culture

It is clear how attitudes, the thinking patterns of individuals, direct the behaviour that they demonstrate. The alignment model holds true where the system it describes is a single person. However, the great power and versatility of this model means that it can also be used to predict the behaviour of organisations, and to help diagnose dysfunction. In these circumstances, we need to understand the organisational equivalents of beliefs, values and identity. How do these concepts bridge across to the collective thinking within organisations, the stuff that creates culture?

■ Organisational values

It is commonplace today to find explicit reference to the values which organisations seek to uphold in the activities of their people. Framed and hung on the wall, or repeated in workshops and communications 'To all employees', these values apply to everyone. The leaders of the organisation expect that they will be interpreted in the daily activity of the various different roles that make up the company's work. We applaud the intention that has gone into these developments, and we have seen excellent examples where the links between behaviour and espoused values are evident and aligned. We have also witnessed many less excellent examples with the kind of misalignments that hit you square in the face as incongruities between talking, thinking and action. There are a few key points to observe in setting an organisation-wide approach here.

Are the values used as a reference in daily discussion?

If the values can be used to help determine the correct choices to be made then they are serving their purpose of ensuring consistent behaviour of a certain type across the organisation. Consider what is happening if the values are not explicitly used in discussions between people. Either individuals can be considered to have sufficiently internalised the values that their decision making will be unconsciously led by the company values, or individuals' own values will be in use, to other and different effect. In addition to this, verbalising things that are important to you helps to bring these things into daily reality.

If I take issue with the quality of product my team is delivering, and feel a sense of dissatisfaction, there are a number of ways in which I can respond to this feeling. One way is to deal with the specific issue, the quality of the product, and suggest ways of making improvements. Another way, and we strongly suggest that this is a far superior way, is to start by referring to the team's values such as high standards, team support and integrity. Then I can explain why the product quality is such a priority issue because it threatens our values, and that immediate support should be put to strengthening the integrity and standards relevant to all the stakeholders connected with this product. This is the way values are put to practical use.

Are the values acknowledged by all?

Our experience shows that people can only acknowledge organisational values and prepare to use them if they understand what the implications of the values are in action. Signing up to a value of service means nothing if I can rationalise that my job is answering the phone anyway. 'That's service so I must be OK.' The effect of values on behaviour is where their worth is measured. Here is where attention is needed; professionalism is not enough. Each member of my team needs to make the connection between professionalism and his own job. One way to facilitate this is to ask people to list all the ways they can think of in which they can be professional, and articulate each example to some level of detail. Without this some people may think that wearing a smart suit is professional, while others will make different kinds of associations.

> The effect of values on behaviour is where their worth is measured.

What rules accompany the values?

Individual interpretations aside, are there any rules which the whole company must share if everyone is to know that its values are being preserved? For example, in our own company one of our values concerns the designing of creative and innovative solutions for our clients, and this is bound by a number of rules. These include:

- that we work with the client's possibilities for innovation, not our own
- that all innovative solutions must also deliver effective and measurable results
- that we act as role models in creative thinking whenever we are with clients.

These are just some of the rules which help us to express the value we attach to being creative and innovative. During our account management meetings we share the ways in which we have been able to do this and thus we have a measure. We also have methods to get feedback from our clients as an external check.

Spend a moment reflecting on the answers to these questions:

1 Does your organisation have a set of values? If so, what are they?

_____

_____

2 Are the values used as a reference in daily discussion?

_____

_____

3 Are the values acknowledged by all?

_____

_____

4 What rules accompany the values?

_____

_____

■ Organisational beliefs

We discussed beliefs as things about which we feel certain. In an organisational context, culture will be shaped by the things about which people feel certain, and this can vary across a whole range of thinking, from what it is appropriate to wear through to the norms of time keeping and attendance. Each of these is an indication of the sort of behaviour members of the organisation think will be praised or scorned by their leaders. How are these feelings of certainty generated in a large group? And how can they be changed?

The alignment model shows us that it is values and beliefs that drive our behaviour, and a useful way of understanding the connection is to regard beliefs as the glue that holds values in place. Dissolving the glue would mean the value was untethered in our thinking. So, if this is the nature of beliefs, why do we decide upon particular beliefs?

The story of IBM's rise and fall is well-known. IBM had established itself as the world leader in business computing across the world. It had the major share in most markets, and if you were an IT director during the 1970s and 1980s a catch phrase you would know only too well was, 'You won't be sacked for buying IBM'. During this time IBM was the unquestionable giant of computing. Such was the global might of the company that its own collective beliefs about its market domination, elite professional status and impenetrable product spread created an inward-looking complacency. This inward focus allowed Bill Gates to snatch the one product that would secure Microsoft's future and sow the seeds for IBM's downward rollercoaster ride.

Beliefs are truths or rules we erect to be consistent in our actions. The ways in which we behave in order to be consistent with our values and beliefs has been well-documented. Once committed to a purpose, our behaviour becomes increasingly consistent as we act to fulfil that purpose. In IBM's case the consistency created by collective organisational beliefs and values became wholly inappropriate for its future success in the emerging world occupied by young, intelligent and perceptive college graduates, carving their careers in the exciting world of microcomputing.

> Beliefs are truths or rules we erect to be consistent in our actions.

■ Organisational identity

The way an organisation articulates its identity to employees, to its customers and to the public at large will greatly influence its activities, and therefore its results. Let us consider some recent examples. Ciba has a new way of describing itself, no longer a chemicals company, or even a speciality chemicals company, but alongside its logo of the butterfly is stated, 'The company that's transforming the speciality chemical sector – value beyond chemistry.' Xerox, in adapting to the concept of the paperless office now clearly states that it is 'The Document Company', thus changing the emphasis from paper to documents. Dupont creates 'Better things for better living.' NatWest is 'More than just a bank.' Microsoft asks 'Where do you want to go today?' BT is 'Changing the way we work.' The possibilities being opened up by new technology are creating a world in which anything can happen. New paradigms of business are being created every day such that nothing can be taken for granted. We learned as much from IBM's experience during the 1970s and 1980s.

> New paradigms of business are being created every day such that nothing can be taken for granted.

We are living in an age of rapid identity change in commercial and technological markets, and this is putting demands on people working in those markets to be as equally adaptable across a range of identities. In the first half of this century it was sufficient to be good at one thing, be that accounting, bricklaying, mining, plumbing or carpentry. Any of these skills would stand a person in good stead for a lifelong career. In the second half of the century we are experiencing rapid redundancy in the skills we learn, such that it is becoming the norm to learn completely new sets of skills to meet the demand created by technological progress. And so, as organisations recreate their identities, people working in organisations must choose either to adapt their identity as required, or to take advantage of what is happening and proactively develop the flexibility to shape their own future. The latter requires the questioning of closely held values and beliefs, and the open-mindedness quickly to acquire whatever identity may be most appropriate for a particular situation.

Alfred North Whitehead the philosopher pointed out in 1931, that it was appropriate to define education as a process of transmitting what is known only when the time-span of major cultural change was greater than the lifespan of individuals. Under this condition, what people learn in their youth will remain valid and useful for the rest of their lives. But: 'We are living in the first period in human history for which this assumption is false ... today this time-span is considerably shorter than that of human life, and accordingly our training must prepare individuals to face a novelty of conditions.' Education, therefore, must now be defined as a lifelong process of continuing enquiry. And so the most important learning of all – for both children and adults – is learning how to learn, acquiring the skills of self-directed inquiry.[3]

Organisational identity is crucially important as an anchor for alignment. Employees will naturally align themselves to the corporate identity, or to their perception of it, serving the master as it were, and the way in which they do this will depend on the degree to which the other distinctions in the universal alignment model are being attended to. A well-formed organisational identity must therefore be shaped from an understanding of purpose and an informed perception of the external system, the market and industry, in which the organisation is operating, and the possibilities which that perception offers. An absence of this high-level identity often results in pockets of different identities in the company, like mini-cultures, each one focusing in on itself, seeking a common purpose, identity and attitudes. This is more commonly known as 'group-think'.

If you defined the identity of your organisation by metaphor, what would it be? Use a comparison to some other figure or object that resonates with the sense you have of the organisation in which you work, a well-oiled machine, a slumbering giant or pick and mix sweet counter, for instance.

Here's a quick organisational and personal audit questionnaire. How aligned are your attitudes with the collective attitudes of your organisation?

Complete the following statements both for yourself and for your perception of the collective attitudes of the organisation. Some people find it easier to begin with beliefs and work upwards to identity. You may find that two, three or more iterations are needed to articulate your true thoughts and feelings.

Identity

This organisation's identity is:

My identity is:

Values

As an organisation we value:

My values in connection with my role in the organisation are:

Beliefs

As an organisation we believe:

My beliefs in connection with my role in the organisation are:

Now consider what evidence exists to support these beliefs

Organisational beliefs:

Personal beliefs:

Changing attitudes

We have noted the importance of values, beliefs and identity for individuals and for groups, teams and organisations. We have talked about the way these can operate in an unconscious fashion, determining our responses to the world without passing through our conscious attention. We hope that the reflection encouraged earlier in this chapter will help you to begin to recognise the different elements of attitude which exist in your thinking. The process of bringing these thoughts into your conscious is, in itself, very useful. Awareness is the first step toward exerting some control over these, the drivers of our behaviour.

> **Beliefs only exist where there is evidence to support them.**

One of the questions that all of this discussion begs is this: how can we change the different elements of attitude? Given the importance that this part of our thinking has in determining our outcomes we would be well-advised to find and then grasp the levers which control changes here. We want to provide some advice and guidelines, both for you as an individual, and for you acting at group level in your organisation. These thoughts will be a helpful companion in your alignment activities. They are not a complete recipe for changing thinking patterns – we do not wish to give the impression that this is always a simple and easy process. Methods vary. While at one end of the spectrum there is the power of positive thinking, a simple universal aid for everyone, the other end is more complex. This is the territory of psychology and psychotherapy, and beyond the scope of this book.

■ Personal changes

Beliefs

Beliefs only exist where there is evidence to support them. Changing beliefs which you no longer wish to hold can start by gathering counterevidence, that is, any evidence, from your own or other people's perceptions, that might disprove your belief. This involves gathering feedback from others, challenging your own assumptions and reevaluating information as if it might have different meanings.

> **To build new and empowering beliefs be more positive with your language.**

'I'm not very good at influencing people' would be an inhibiting belief for many people in business today, and this might be how some actually think at present. By seeking out the real-life instances of where they did influence someone, maybe in a different context or a different place, they can begin to break the hold that the old belief had for them.

To build new and empowering beliefs be more positive with your language. Try saying, 'I am getting ever better at influencing people.' We also need to gather the evidence, from specific instances, which supports the belief. Like a chair on which we can rest, a belief works best when it is stable, and for this it needs a number of legs. Consider that you might want at least four good legs, or solid references of evidence, to start to change how you think.

Values

The impact of values depends much on the importance of each relative to the others. One route to change, therefore, is to list our values as a hierarchy, and identifying those which feel most important. This will allow us to see where conflict can occur. For example, if you want to enjoy a greater sense of health and well-being, yet find that you rate health as only your seventh most important value behind work, success and wealth etc., you have found some important clues. The drive to work hard, be successful and earn money may well mean you have to make more hours at the office a priority ahead of a daily trip to the gym.

If you were to imagine elevating that value to a higher position in your own value hierarchy you will begin, consciously at first, to give it greater emphasis. Make values a part of your everyday thinking, a yardstick for your own behaviour and a guide to making important decisions. It will be a significant improvement in situations where your autopilot was engaged without your knowing what course it was steering. So rewrite the hierarchy in a new order. Give it frequent consideration. Think through the implications. Use your values as an aid at times of decision and choice. By all of these actions you can begin to change your values, and shape your future.

> Use your values as an aid at times of decision and choice ... change your values, and shape your future.

Identity

Identity is most easily thought of in metaphor for many people. And in the world of metaphor we can play any games we want. Today I can act as if I am anyone I want to be, I think of myself in new and enabling ways. No one else need know that I am imagining myself with attributes of someone I admire, a real or mythical role model. I can simply pretend that I already have any capabilities I wish to acquire or develop. The mind is a wonderful tool for this. We are what we think we can be. Try it and see.

■ Organisational changes

Gaining consensus in a group of people about any aspects of attitude requires deliberate discussion. This is often missed in organisations, so the attitude or culture which prevails is the one which grows into this void. More purposefully to shape the way people think requires two things as a minimum:

1 Encouragement of a deliberate and focused discussion for all about the values, identity or the culture of the group in which you work. Ask people for ideas and suggestions. How would they like it to be, and what ideas do they have for achieving that?
2 Leaders need to walk their talk. Attitudes are borne out by what people do, not by what they say.

This complex subject, changing attitudes in an organisation, is dealt with in more detail in later chapters of the book. Our intention here has been to establish the connection between attitudes and action, and relate this to the universal alignment model.

Notes

1 Robert B Cialdini (1993) *Influence, Science and Practice*. HarperCollins.
2 Anthony Robbins (1992) *Awaken the Giant Within*. Simon & Schuster.
3 Malcolm Knowles (1990) *The Adult Learner – A Neglected Species*. Gulf Publishing.

5

ENVIRONMENT

Introduction

Earlier in the book we delved into some aspects of environment, the physical domain of an organisation – what we see, hear, smell, taste and feel, or if you like, the capsule of external sensory experience in which the transference of thoughts into visible action takes place. In this chapter we put our environment more closely under the microscope.

What is environment?

In the universal alignment model the environment provides the context where attitudes are formed, and where people express themselves through action. You could say that the workplace is an arena for the expression of human thought and feeling. Ideally, the environment will foster and promote desirable behaviour to fulfil a specific purpose. As humans we are able to make choices about shaping our environment in any number of possible ways. All other creatures on this earth must adapt. So we must therefore accept responsibility for what we create, both the environment itself, and the outputs generated from it. Do you remember the polar bears mentioned earlier? Humans created their caged environment, and the bears adapted to it. The output was to condition the bears' physical movement, restricting them to a few steps in either direction, even after being released into a much larger enclosure. Environmentalists can give endless accounts of our irresponsible actions in generating negative outputs from the environments we create. Forest demolition in Papua New Guinea and other parts of the world is but one example of the downside of our impact on the environment. The unconsidered consequences created by evolving humans acting on the environment are now of global concern for the survival of the human race.

Let us focus on a modern institution catering for an inveterate human tendency – the gambling casino. The purpose of the casino is to profit from people who are willing to take risks with their money. The environment created by the positioning of gaming tables, croupiers, machines, mirrors, cameras and other security devices promote the operation of certain rules and conventions. The decor and climate will suggest the wealth that can be realised by winning, and there will be an absence in the physical domain of anything associated with losing. The gambling devices and systems are designed to ensure that, overall, casinos makes money. Although customers may perceive an element of randomness, or luck, casino rules and conventions assure predictability, and the output is profit. But sometimes there are undesired outputs such as cheating, drunkenness, bankruptcy and debt. These are outputs that make an impact on the casino's profits and image, as well as on the human beings involved. Casinos may produce rich people, but they also produce poverty, cheating and desolation.

> The history of human innovation, in shaping the environment, reveals a consistent lack of attention to ecology – an ignorance or neglect of those actions we perform in the name of progress.

Consider the automobile. The desired output is a flexible, comfortable, convenient and effective mode of travel. But, in creating the environment to achieve that, with the internal combustion engine and a complex network of highways, we also get a great many undesired outputs such as road rage, congestion, pollution, accidents and terrible deaths. In fact, the imbalance between desired and undesired behaviour, for many people, has negated the intended benefit of such a flexible system of travel. Indeed, it has, in many places, become very inflexible.

The history of human innovation, in shaping the environment, reveals a consistent lack of attention to ecology – an ignorance or neglect of those actions we perform in the name of progress. Think about the millennium computer bug. During the last ten years of the twentieth century we have lacked the foresight to build a simple function into computer systems to deal with a four-digit number. What does this say about our concern for the future, or our ability to imagine reality any further than a few years beyond the present?

So what hope does this offer for the future of work organisations? We are beginning to face the reality of what has been known for thousands of years, that the environment we create for ourselves has wider influences, both on ourselves, and on many other factors of which we may not be aware. The imbalance in global trade and labour is never designed by intention, but arises as a consequence of world economic and social policies. The consequences of any environmental change will always have unintended consequences, perhaps not immediately – some feedback loops take time to have an effect. There exists today a wide range of beliefs about the best environment for organisational success, and there is much contention among the ideologists.

The quality of care in the UK health service, for example, deteriorated after the government altered the environment by introducing a huge burden of administrative responsibility. The desired output of increased efficiency was not achieved. Undesired outputs included an increase in workload and high stress among professional medical staff. In the workplace more generally there seems to be an abundance of customer dissatisfaction, low motivation, reduced effort, accidents, absenteeism, sickness, low staff retention, suppressed energy and a lack of creative ideas – all undesirable outputs. It is about time we began applying the intelligence we credit ourselves with to create more ecological ways, ways of organising our environment for the good of both commerce and humanity.

Culture and perception

All environments change – time sees to that. But even the most progressive creators of the future will resist change to some degree, because it is a basic human instinct to do so. Environments are created by people to produce specific results, and this, in turn, means that the routines which make up workplace behaviour form a culture which becomes self-reinforcing. If you use the roads you will conform to a culture defined by the highway code, because there are unwanted consequences if you do not. This system is self-reinforcing for most people, and the law is there to punish those who break the code. Mihaly Csikszentmihalyi[1] describes culture this way: 'Cultures are defensive constructions against chaos, designed to reduce the impact of randomness on experience.' To some, rules may be perceived as tedious, but without them life would become inversely tedious through the need to recreate procedures for helping us through daily routines. Environments, therefore, contain factors designed to support a set of rules and conventions with the intention of reducing randomness and increasing predictability. Some people are comfortable with this, others want to break the rules. This is how progress occurs, by struggling with the dichotomy of human preference. The human race is a mix of conformists, radicals and all shades in between.

> 'Cultures are defensive constructions against chaos, designed to reduce the impact of randomness on experience'. [Mihaly Csikszentmihalyi]

■ Systems thinking

There have been many recent developments, in all areas of science, towards a more holistic, ecological or systemic view of life in general.[2] The common hypothesis is that all living organisms have the ability to think and make decisions. An organism's responses to feedback loops create changes that lead to the development and evolution of the organism. Attempts to understand these changes require a systemic focus, not on the way a particular component of an organism works, but on relationships:

- between each component's process
- with the entire organism
- with its environment.

Living organisms are self-organising, and they remain in a state of equilibrium unless they are made unstable by an abrupt change somewhere in the system. These changes occur from adaptive responses to the organism's environment.

The focus on relationships is a significant change to the way scientists are analysing organic systems, and it provides a useful parallel for understanding organisational development, the main difference being that humans have the capacity to create the environment as well as adapt to it. Organisations are living organisms made up of numbers of people who think and make decisions. Some people instinctively follow rules, preferring to adapt slowly to environmental changes, while others look for ways of breaking the rules, creating new environments in markets, technologies or work processes for example. Feedback loops exist in the organisational system in many forms, and responses to feedback determine future success. If the responses are appropriate, the organisation becomes more aligned with its purpose, and its environment will reflect this through enhanced organisation of processes. If, however, responses are inappropriate, the organisation may become unstable and this will be reflected in the environment by increasing amounts of disorder and chaos.

When we examined the components of performance, and the possible feedback loops, we introduced four metaphors. The hamster wheel fits with rule followers, while game strategy may result in some new rules being formed, but with only slight deviations from existing rules. Mission impossible is clearly a rule maker, but you have to go to superheroes to find the major league rule breakers. On an organisational level no better example can be found than the Virgin Group which is competing with many large and well-established companies such as British Airways and Coca-Cola. More recently, the financial sector has Richard Branson to contend with. When you look at companies that innovate you find the rule breakers and rule makers, people who shape environments for themselves and others. Like any other organism, a commercial organisation must respond appropriately to its feedback loops, breaking and making rules that help it to align with its purpose and its environment. The type of response made to any particular feedback loop depends very much on how the organisation thinks and makes decisions.

■ Personalised versions of reality

Figure 5.1 shows very simply the way in which we respond to and influence the environment. The inferences we draw from what goes on around us will form memories of our experience. These memories will consist of generalisations, distortions and deletions – that is how the mind works. We attach meanings to our experience, and by doing so we create our own personalised version of reality.

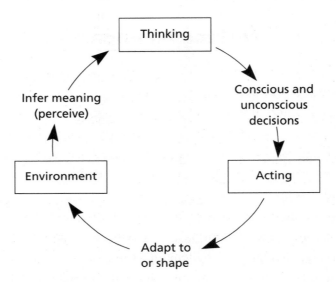

Figure 5.1 Effect of perception and decision making on the environment

Imagine two people attending the same seminar. It is doubtful that both will come away with the same perceptions, meanings and attitudes, even though they were both in the same place at the same time, exposed to the same sensory information. At school, I would stare out of the window while imagining the scenes portrayed by my teacher. Unfortunately, the meaning my teacher put on this behaviour was 'not listening'. On the contrary, I was listening and forming visual images of my understanding. One person's meaning can be far from another's, and this has a major impact on the forming of our perceptions. It is like the optimist: she has a half-full glass. The pessimist has a half-empty glass. One of the elements in the creation of our perceptions is the language we use to describe events and situations to ourselves – our self-talk. I can tell myself that the boss is angry with me, or that the boss has a red face and is shouting. The boss may be angry with himself, but looking at me at the same time, or he could have just been ditched by his lover, or his dog may have been run over, or he may have been disciplined by his boss, or any one of numerous other possible meanings.

Beware – perceptions distort reality!

Beware – perceptions distort reality!

Making an impact

Once our perceptions are formed we use them to decide how to act. Some of our actions will be guided by an unconscious decision, and others by more conscious thought-out decisions. The most effective learning is done consciously, that is, we apply the full capacity of the neo-cortex, or intellectual thinking part of our brain to form perceptions from experience. The next stage is to make decisions.

Continuing this process we have a choice of staying within conventions and rules (adapting), or having a different impact by modifying, changing or challenging conventions (shaping). If our perceptions are free of contamination from false meanings, and if we have a sensible handle on the bigger picture of goals and mission, we are more likely to follow this with appropriate decisions and effective action. One important aspect in the forming of our decisions is our capability to recognise and evaluate behavioural patterns. These are the indicators of change in an organisation, and they provide vital clues to the state of alignment and whether or not there is any change taking place.

I am reminded of a courageous and insightful manager called Frank whom I had the pleasure to meet at a recent seminar we were running on the subject 'Alignment and Change'. We were talking about cultural change, and how people perceive their environment, and Frank recounted to us a time when he was recruited into a company in the role of department manager, a post previously held by a strict authoritarian. After spending some time listening and observing patterns of behaviour in the environment, Frank became aware of how people had adapted to a tight command and control style of management. He realised that an abrupt action was needed, a kind of statement to the effect that things were going to change.

Frank didn't follow convention by holding a meeting, sending an email or a memo, or organising a conference. Instead, he did something so different that it made an immediate impact on the way people perceived their relationship with management. He enlisted the help of three employees to help him carry his desk, a historic symbol of authority, out to some waste ground near the carpark. He then let it be known by informal means that the following day he would be ceremoniously burning it. Over 50 people turned up to watch and photograph Frank cremating all the associations employees had made with the authority imposed by the previous department manager. Frank followed this by making further changes to the environment, including the introduction of open plan desk arrangements, improved decoration, more round tables for informal meetings and an area for relaxation. These changes were consistent with the changes he was to bring to the style of management and leadership in the department.

A living environment – mirror to culture

An organisation's environment reveals much about the organisation, and about the people holding the power within it. You may have experienced the incongruent company that says one thing and acts in an entirely different manner. It is possible to talk about people being the most important asset, or quality being a way of life, or innovation being the key to success. Platitudes abound and grow bolder. In a public bar near our office there is a mission statement on the wall 'to meet our customers' future expectations now'. They must have some kind of crystal ball to see that far ahead, yet my current expectations still fail to be met as I queue patiently at the bar waiting to be served.

> An organisation's environment reflects much about the organisation, and about the people holding the power within it.

There is nothing wrong with mission statements on the wall, or quality rosettes in reception, as long as the behaviours they allude to are congruent with the messages they exude. Environments reflect culture like a mirror. They are formed by the culture. It is a self-fulfilling prophecy that whatever is believed by the people with power will prevail, regardless of motivational pictures on the wall and metaphoric decor. If you really believe in quality then that belief will permeate your life and will be evident in the environment you create. A company which is fully congruent with its espoused value for innovation will integrate innovation into its environment in active ways rather than resorting to decorative platitudes as part of its strategy to become innovative.

> Environments reflect culture like a mirror.

A superb example of this is provided by a company called Oticon, based in Copenhagen. It has earned the name 'spaghetti culture' because of its lack of job titles and desks, plus flexible working hours. Its environment supports the cultural beliefs to the extent that a clear plastic tube has been installed from the shredding machine on the top floor, projecting down through all the common areas, including rest rooms and reception, to the basement. Wherever you go in the building you are aware of the falling shredded paper as a reminder to abandon the memo in favour of a meeting, and to use technology not paper to manage information. This is an effective example of how an environment has been purposely designed to create change in working patterns. Suggestive posters and statements are not needed if the environment itself symbolises the culture. Oticon could have put up lots of signs suggesting that people use less paper and meet more often. Instead, it attached the belief to the process of shredding, and integrated that into the environment.

Patterns of behaviour and the environment

The environment is where the indicators of change can be observed. It is the arena where the transformation of thinking patterns into behavioural patterns occurs. Think about patterns for a while. Consider a theme park with exciting rides and the changing patterns of moving people during the period of a day. At certain times you might hear screaming rise to peak levels, and you would see large groups moving here and there forming queues for the various attractions. Gatherings around cafés and restaurants would grow at lunchtime. The way the park is laid out and organised will determine these patterns. Anywhere where people gather there are patterns of behaviour influenced by the particular environment they are in.

The environment is where the indicators of change can be observed.

What patterns can you notice in your organisation? To what extent are the patterns influenced by the environment? If you were to audit your environment what would you say about the various aspects?

- Space

  _____

  _____

- Proximity of people to each other

  _____

  _____

- Light

  _____

  _____

- Sound

  _____

  _____

- Smells and tastes

  _____

  _____

- Equipment

  _____

  _____

- Facilities

  _____

  _____

- Decor

  _____

  _____

- Furniture

  _____

  _____

- Behaviour

  _____

  _____

- Other

  _____

  _____

In what way do these aspects of your environment reflect your organisation's espoused values and beliefs? What does the environment say about your company's identity? Do any of these aspects enhance or limit the capability of your people? If you were to change anything, what would you change and why? What would encourage desired behaviours and what would reduce undesired behaviours? To what extent do people adapt to the environment provided, and how often do people reshape it?

Some years ago I was asked to help improve the service in one region of a UK field service operation. I noticed all the managers, team leaders and work schedulers were in separate rooms. There was no common big picture showing the state of service calls and engineers' locations, resulting in duplication of effort and a compartmentalised approach to work. This was in the days before hand-held communication devices were a common tool for the service engineer. The very first thing we did was to knock down three walls and create a common area, the central focus being a large map and T-card system showing current status of calls and engineers. Once we had finished shaping a more appropriate environment, one that suggested a high value for service quality, the team was able to change work patterns and improve service levels. The original compartmentalised environment was a response to increasing customer demands, and the true intention of the team's response was not to improve customer service, but to bring personal relief from the growing chaos.

So, when you are thinking about your own personal environment, that of your team, or your entire organisation, you have many indicators available to you to suggest whether change might be appropriate. Look around and notice the patterns of behaviour keeping the environment the way it is.

Try this simple exercise. In your mind, make some changes to the fabric of the building, move walls, change furniture, change the colour, light and space. When you have finished making changes imagine people coming in to the building. How will this environment change what they do and how they do it? Will this challenge their thinking in some way? How will they respond? How could they respond? You might of course go one step further and make the changes a reality, then stand back and watch what happens.

Aligning at any level, attitudes, capability or action, will necessarily change the environment in some way. Very often it is a change in the environment that indicates an alignment has taken place. Reshaping an environment does not necessarily result in improvements, while merely adapting is more likely to lead to extinction as your competitors take over. The key to successful shaping is having other people with you who are willing and determined to make the shaping work. A company made up entirely of rule breakers will create chaos and disorder before eventually collapsing. Adapters are critically important to ensuring processes are organised so as to optimise the benefits from innovative ideas. This is a vital point which will be covered further in later chapters. We all have the choice, as we observe the patterns, to shape or adapt.

> We all have the choice, as we observe the patterns, to shape or adapt.

> For an organisation to compete it must both shape its environment, and adapt its processes accordingly.

For an organisation to compete it must both shape its environment, and adapt its processes accordingly. The degree of success it achieves will be determined by the appropriateness of the responses to feedback from the environment. The environment in an organisation reflects its culture and makes a statement about its congruity with espoused values and beliefs. Changes to environments have ecological impact on systems outside the organisation, and some take time to feed back into the originating system. When considering any aligning action therefore, the environment is a critical consideration, not just for the immediate organisation and its employees, but for much wider environmental connections.

Notes

1 Mihaly Csikszentmihalyi (1992) *Flow, The Psychology of Happiness*. Rider.
2 Fritjof Capra (1996) *The Web of Life*. HarperCollins.

Part 2

ALIGNMENT APPLIED

6

A PRELUDE TO ALIGNMENT IN ORGANISATIONS

- **Introduction**
- **Leadership**
- **Teams**
- **Innovation**
- **Managing change**

Introduction

Organisations in most spheres of activity face a huge array of issues and a bewildering pace of change today. It is no longer possible to design structures and methods around steady-state operating. This is perhaps the first generation of management that has had to deal with continual transition, and it is having to learn the lessons while steering business through a considerable range of complex challenges. In a world where change is the only constant, and where solutions are infinite in number, shape, form and sophistication, being 'in control' is taking on new meaning and presenting new challenges. In times long past, the job of managing people and resources was relatively simple: managers were expected to make the rules and enforce them. Today it is far less clear what the rules are, and whether, indeed, certain rules are a good or bad thing. As soon as a decision on management approach and style is adopted someone will break that mould and suggest a new one with convincing need and utility. And so the wheels of progress continue to turn, often creating increasing demands and stresses on managements looking for stability, substance and order.

> It is no longer possible to design structures and methods around steady-state operating.

The response of business leaders is crucial, the effort applied to equipping organisations is in many cases laudable. We have restructured, downsized, reengineered, focused on quality and empowered our people. Each of these, as responses to the environment in which we find ourselves operating, has served a useful purpose in the moment of its application.

It is not our intention here to provide yet another stock response, another recipe for success in today's circumstances. Rather, we offer some well-tried principles which we suggest might underpin the response that managers choose in any particular set of circumstances. Principles serving as a guide rather than a ten-point universal remedy.

Our experience is that organisations are focusing energy in four major ways to improve their ability to prosper in current circumstances, and to shape up for the future.

Leadership

A new interest has arisen in the subject of leadership. Of course, in every situation, in every company, it is true to say that leadership is vital, and "twas ever thus'. Yet organisations are returning to the study of leadership to see how they can better equip the men and women they elect as their leaders. This is not so simple today with changing social attitudes of a modern workforce. The new generation of employee expects much more from the employer than ever before. Changes in demographics, the proliferation of technology, and the globalisation of international business are just some of the dynamics making life in organisations increasingly more complex. This complexity brings unprecedented demands on those entrusted with leadership. Perhaps aware of the failings of leadership development in the past, maybe conscious of specific new elements of challenge facing leaders today or merely awake to the importance of leadership to this generation, it is certainly a hot topic once again.

Teams

The concept of the team is now widely accepted as *the* key aspect of an organised workforce. And teams come in many guises: project teams, self-directed teams, self-managed teams, quality teams, to draw upon just some of the new terminology used to describe the ways in which people come together to work. The trend is to shift power, authority, responsibility and decision making from individual managers to teams, thus increasing the flexibility of the organisation. This is to be heralded as a move towards a more humane system of working, recognising the natural creativity released when hearts and minds are free from authoritarian constraint. Through our consulting work we have experienced a number of companies achieving remarkable results with teams.

We are also aware of many other companies for whom team-working is either unrecognised or has been interpreted in ways that suppress energy rather than stimulate it.

Not all teams are effective – some are teams by name only, their output being little more than the sum of each individual's contribution. True teams have a dynamic energy, generated from a freedom of will which can create many times the sum of each individual's performance. The jewel in the crown of high performance teams is not so much the hard and quantifiable results, but the creative ideas and innovative solutions that help to shape the future for the organisation.

> It is now apparent that developing and successfully exploiting new ideas is a vital capability to master for every organisation.

Innovation

If leadership is a hot topic today, so too is innovation. Once regarded as an optional extra for technology-based companies, a new understanding is emerging. It is now apparent that developing and successfully exploiting new ideas is a vital capability to master for every organisation. And this is true not just where the output is a new product or service, for innovation proves to be equally valuable as a way of improving the production process, the supply chain or a support function. A growing number of companies are bringing innovation alive, stretching the boundaries of possibility to create commercial and operational environments that will secure their future prosperity.

> Mastering change unlocks all future possibilities.

Managing change

The fourth response we observe among business thinkers is to seek to learn how to manage change within organisations. This still moves more management tomes off the shelves than any other subject and remains the focus of research work at schools and universities around the world, yet there is still no single right answer. So the promise remains the same. Mastering change unlocks all future possibilities.

In the chapters that follow we intend to offer some thoughts and share some experience of approaches which are based around the alignment model. We believe that this, plus a core set of principles, some of which were outlined earlier in the book, can guide a highly effective response to the world in which we live. We will take a closer look at principles, and how they can help an organisation to keep aligned with its purpose in Chapter 11, but first the four main areas of focus – leadership, teams, innovation and change, warrant further exploration.

7

LEADERSHIP

Introduction

We have just had the privilege of working with a major UK government department to help it redefine leadership and to reappraise how it develops and encourages leaders. Faced with considerable challenges by the environment in which it operates and by its political masters, this department has decided that leadership is one of the keys to the achievement of the vision laid down by its chief.

We consulted widely with senior managers, and we shared the output of extensive enquiry among the bulk of the population of over 20,000 people. We exposed the senior managers to different models of leadership; we helped them to envisage the type of leadership required in their particular context; we provoked them to identify the strengths and shortfalls of their current leadership style. In a lengthy series of drafts and redrafts we worded as precise a description of leadership as we could while trying to meet the needs of all interested parties. For all the effort that went into this description it is glaringly obvious that the value of the exercise six months, one year or two years further on has little to do with words.

What is leadership?

Leadership is about doing, and is apparent only through the realm of action. Fine words, statements of importance and corporate communication strategies count for little compared to the visible behaviour of the most influential people in the organisation, those who already occupy the role of leaders. Leadership can be studied by those who are interested, it can be trained in those who wish to improve their own performance. We can select those with experience and spot those with potential. Yet the test of leadership is more than a tick in the box for leadership competence. Leaders need to do more than occupy high office and wield their power. Effective leadership is an activity, and one which requires an align-

> **Leadership is about doing, and is apparent only through the realm of action.**

ment of action with attitudes and purpose if the desired results are to be obtained.

The action elements of leadership are well-understood. They have been debated and catalogued extensively by every generation since the ancient Greeks first tried to systemise the selection of military leaders. Indeed, it is only in the last 20 years that business has been able to shake off the legacy of military thinking and begin to form its own view of what leadership means. But that is another story.

> Effective leadership is an activity, and one which requires an alignment of action with attitudes and purpose if the desired results are to be obtained.

We know that leaders provide vision, inspire others, listen, motivate and encourage. They make decisions, communicate and represent their teams. They focus on task completion, draw out individual contribution and guide team processes to good effect. These things we recognise, and it appears to be relatively simple, at first sight, to expect this of the people we put into leadership roles.

What of the capability of leadership? What is the potential required of leaders in order for them to be successful? The attributes of leaders have been extensively researched and documented. It can become something of a parlour game to assemble the definitive list of leadership qualities: charisma, courage, determination, stamina, far-sightedness, vision, wisdom and more have all been listed by various experts over the years.

More recently the systematic identification of competence profiles has spawned numerous attempts to isolate the essence of leadership. It remains true that whatever the capabilities of leaders, they are only visible through action. And we need to know to what extent that potential which has not yet been made visible can be identified and tapped. One of the most pervasive beliefs we find as we run our leadership workshops is that leaders are born not made, and that these capabilities cannot really be trained into people. This belief holds a clue to the question, because it reminds us of the importance of belief. Let us explore the other alignment distinctions to see what light they shed on the matter.

Clouds on the leadership horizon

For us the puzzle of leadership begins to unravel only when we start to understand the attitudes that drive it. Every leader will have values and beliefs, influenced by personality and the conditioning that has shaped her make-up, that is, the clouds obscuring the horizons of capability. Very often values will be unconsciously held – we literally do not know what drives us sometimes. And as we will see, values that seem only indirectly relevant to our pursuit of leadership can have more leverage than we might guess.

Is it at all possible to be a truly effective leader in the context of organised labour if you place no value upon the contribution of your team mates? Absolutely not, we are sure that everyone will agree. There will be few who would declare that they do not value the contribution of others. But is this sufficient? If we value the contribution of others very highly then it is likely that we will allow them the time, space and resources to try out new and different ideas. By the same token, we have worked with managers who are sincere when they say that they value their team members, and continue to dictate and direct, thereby limiting the contribution these valued assets can make to the business. So perhaps it is not enough to place value on the contribution of others; maybe we need to elevate this in our values hierarchy above the ranking that we give to our need to be in control. If the control value wins out and remains more important for us, then consciously or unconsciously, by hook or by crook, we will ensure that we retain control at the expense of unlocking the contribution of our team.

Many of our values arise from our social conditioning. The images and ideas that the current generation of managers has grown up with contain many stereotypes of leadership. In his excellent book, *New Leadership for Women and Men*, Michael Simmons[1] detailed some of the aspects of this familiar paradigm of leadership and he identifies some of the assumptions upon which this is based. These assumptions can be rationally dismissed without much trouble, we can declare them a nonsense, but so insidious are they that we might not have escaped their influence completely. To what extent have you or I unconsciously adopted the assumption that people must be controlled, disciplined and externally motivated in order to commit to the organisation and work hard? Do we ever act as if this is true? I, for one, must admit that all too often I do. Good intentions declared consciously are not always sufficient on their own to overcome the effects of other values, unconsciously held, more highly ranked in our hierarchy of importance.

> To what extent have you or I unconsciously adopted the assumption that people must be controlled, disciplined and externally motivated in order to commit to the organisation and work hard?

Linked to this assumption about the nature of people are some assumptions about the role of a manager. Managers have to know best, to be experts. They need to take decisions about what other people will do. And, of course, managers get to pronounce on the capability, contribution and worth (to the organisation) of other people. Do these stereotypical messages fit with the attitudes of enlightened leadership? Not at all, yet they are so ingrained that there are very few managers we have ever met who have escaped their clutches completely. These messages represent a siren voice, calling to our egos, flattering us and making us feel more important, yet luring us into the trap of disempowerment.

What new assumptions would create a world in which people were able to offer a far greater degree of their inherent capability, their human potential? And how would we need to think about leadership in this new world? What is the role of the leader in a collection of able, enthusiastic, empowered people? Perhaps we can even seek out a new metaphor, as Wolfgang did, of ourselves as coaches or enablers where we were once managers and controllers. In whatever way we approach this we begin to see the first steps along the route of leadership development, and before we explore this further, let us briefly consider the higher level of 'purpose'.

Let him who would move the world first move himself. [Seneca]

Purpose and intentions

What is the purpose of a leader? It might well have something to do with getting the job done, meeting targets, driving the business forward. This seems to make a great deal of sense and is certainly in accord with the typical mission seen in annual reports and on the walls of reception at corporate HQ. But, if the most deeply held expression of purpose is the achievement of results, this places results as more important than anything else. Results must be more important than people, not an intended position perhaps, just an unfortunate by-product of the focus on achievement. And then, to some degree at least, we will sacrifice individuals' needs to get the results, probably accepting the right of the leader to be 'right' and allowing his view to be upheld. The consequence then is that the brain that comes free with each pair of hands that we hire will be, to some extent, unemployed.

> If the most deeply held expression of purpose is the achievement of results, this places results as more important than anything else.

As I write this I am experiencing a strong feeling of recognition. Some of the businesses that I have run have been managed with this kind of results-oriented purpose, and hindsight is helping me to understand that this will have been stifling at times. My own focus on results and determination to succeed must have been obvious to the people that I employed, subordinating them, unconsciously but no less certainly, to roles as mere resources in the achievement of my objectives. Sometimes our conscious intentions get overridden by deeper rooted values driving us, perhaps unconsciously, towards results to which we attach a higher priority.

> Sometimes our conscious intentions get overridden by deeper rooted values driving us, perhaps unconsciously, towards results to which we attach a higher priority.

In contrast, in our consultancy, CPS International, we are concerned more with the impact of our work and with building a team of people who want to work together in a common cause. Having a creative and enjoyable environment which nourishes individuals' needs is more important than a simple increment in profitability. We could survive in the former without the latter, and clearly do not want the latter at the expense of the former. It is not that profits are not important, far from it, but the higher value of human respect means that we are learning to be more flexible in how we organise and manage our finances. The consequence of these values is far more space for each of our colleagues to contribute their expertise and ideas, and we hope that, unconsciously as well as consciously, we communicate that we value others highly. Profit growth will certainly follow, but without having obscured our view of purpose.

What we can conclude from this is the importance and deep-rooted influence of our thinking at the levels of identity, value and purpose. I terrifically enjoyed William Byham and Jeff Cox's entertaining book *ZAPP*[2] in which magic access to a twelfth dimension allows managers to see the process of empowerment as a small bolt of blue lightning passing from one person to another. This is a great metaphor for an important aspect of leadership. Without a set of values that allow, nay, even demand, empowerment and inclusion, we remain unlikely to carry out the relatively simple steps required to zapp our colleagues.

■ A common leadership purpose

In one of my previous roles as Training Manager for a large computer company, I was approached by Jeremy, the Quality Manager, asking for a training program to teach managers the ways of quality. 'They aren't taking quality seriously,' he said. In response I enquired 'What is the collective role of managers in this company?' 'I can only answer for myself and my team,' replied Jeremy. 'Then I will ask the MD.' So I called the MD and posed the same question. 'Jeremy wants me to train our managers in the ways of quality, and I need to know what is the collective role of managers in this company?' After some contemplation the MD replied, 'I can only answer for myself and those I am immediately responsible for.

Perhaps you should ask the General Managers this question.' So I did, and back came a similar reply. What became very clear, the more people I approached with this question, was that although each individual manager could answer for herself and her team, whatever common purpose there may have been, binding managers together, it had little to do with quality. This was, we concluded, one of the major reasons why Jeremy was having such a hard time trying to implement a quality strategy.

In my experience of consulting, one aspect of organisational life is crystal clear: that leaving leaders to 'figure out the priorities for themselves' is a recipe for cultural dilemma. The larger the organisation, the more likely that it will consist of a number of mini-cultures. There will certainly be professional differences between functions, and where there is a lack of common purpose, at a higher level than professional values, mini-cultures tend to close ranks and look inward. A leader operating within closed ranks is more than likely to be rewarded and recognised from within those ranks, and so this is where her focus will be directed. Bridging across mini-cultures requires a belief in a common purpose, one that is valued more highly than the values of each mini-culture. At the functional level, people have strong values attached to their jobs. The storeman knows how to organise the store. At the cross-functional level leadership beliefs and values attached to co-operation, respect, communication and creativity need to be considered as more important than functional values, so that greater synergy can be put to the purpose of meeting customer needs. This higher purpose will provide an organisation-level focus on what needs to be done to be both effective and successful. One of the truest measures of excellence for an organisation is provided by customer perception.

> One of the truest measures of excellence for an organisation is provided by customer perception.

To see what is
right and not
do it is want
of courage.
[Confucius]

Courage

So where were we on that journey of self-development towards ever better leadership? We can start to accept that the most significant changes are not the sudden adoption of leadership behaviour. The most telling shifts that any leader can make are those which take place out of sight as we adapt and restructure the way in which we think, the values that we hold to support ideal behaviours. In some instances as leaders, for the benefit of the many, we

> Leaders need to be able to suspend habitual responses in favour of the difficult choices demanded of them.

need to act in ways which are not necessarily aligned with our established preferences. First of all, we need to figure this out and decide to take action. Thereafter comes the tough step, doing it, and this takes courage. Leaders need to be able to suspend habitual responses in favour of the difficult choices demanded of them. They need to be able to give honest feedback where it may be difficult for others to accept, and to confront people and issues in the interest of the wider group. Leaders need to take decisions that may disappoint and upset others. One measure of our leadership ability is the degree to which we can summon up the courage to do these things, rather than shy away from them. This same quality of courage is needed in a longer time scale if we are to embark on the journey of self-development. If a leader's purpose is to envision and create the future, then there will be tough choices to make, old values and ideals to challenge, and this is just in dealing with ourselves. This is why it is apparent to more and more people that leadership of ourselves is the first task for those who would lead others.

Leadership within enables leadership without.

Metaphors of leadership

Courageous and effective leaders bring clarity to the ambiguity which is part and parcel of organisational life. That is one aspect of their role, to help others steer the right course through a mixture of weather conditions. But one of the more common ambiguities we have encountered is created by the blurred distinctions often made between management and leadership. On the one hand, business schools teach us the science of business administration, the essence of best practice in management, and on the other hand, we have the visionary gurus who would have us forsake control mechanisms for the inspirational teachings of greater leaders. Creating the right mix might be a simple process were it not for the wide variation of attitudes and capabilities among individuals. In many cases, the responsibility for this mix is delegated to the training and development function. First attend the management course, then the one on leadership. That they are recognised as two entities does not help, and being taught separately leaves individuals to make their own integration of learning. Why have we not invented a new word to combine manager and leader?

> Organisational disease can often be the result of inappropriate perceptions of identity and role.

Surely, anyone responsible for others should be combining both management and leadership skills. The name we use for our role, and how we think about our purpose, has an influence on our sense of identity, and in many ways provides a metaphor for shaping what we actually do. Organisational disease can often be the result of inappropriate perceptions of identity and role. In the prison service there are some warders who believe in punishing criminals, and others who believe in reform. The warder's perception of his role will influence how he communicates with the prisoners. Think about parenting. Some parents restrict a child's freedom, perhaps driven by their role as 'protector', while others will encourage children to explore and discover, driven by a different perception of the parental role. A parent's identity will be formed by multiple roles, and it is the application of values in each specific situation which will determine the behaviour towards the child. However, consistency over time will suggest which role is more dominant. Is the role one of 'nurturer with a lower value for protection', or 'protector with a lower value for nurturing'? The difference between these two orientations will show in the relationship between parent and child.

Should we be leaders who manage or managers who lead? The following true account is rather sad, but serves to demonstrate this point very well.

Recently I was talking with James, an acquaintance of mine, who recounted with great dis-ease a conversation with his CEO which identified one reason why the company he worked for was in debt and losing money rapidly. This story begins with a young trainee called Peter who worked hard as a parks groundsman and studied diligently for a diploma in his own time. James could see great promise in Peter who had a strong flair for landscaping. But what James saw in Peter, in addition to his natural flair for sculpting the earth, was the effect of Peter's energy and enthusiasm on other employees, and so James promoted him to team leader. Peter was highly motivated and keen to establish a management career with the company, but little did he know that a cancer had already taken root. In order to improve the finances, the CEO, an accountant by profession, realised that he could cut payroll costs by including a number of people in a recent deal where a large contract had been lost to a competitor. Peter was to be one of those people, and James recalled with disgust the very words the CEO used as he explained to him 'What a golden opportunity this is to get rid of some people and cut our costs.' I imagine the CEO wasn't aware of the impact this language had on James.

This story is a stark reminder of the damage that can be done through a sense of identity formed from preconditioned thinking. The CEO, perhaps because of his accounting background, perceived his role as a cost cutter, or slave to next month's bottom line figures. This resulted in a stream of damaging moves (or from his perception 'golden opportunities') designed to reduce the company's expense burden, with no concern for developing capability to compete in the long term. There are many tough choices to make in business, and the way a manager or leader perceives her role will have a profound influence on what she will pay attention to, while working through her day-to-day priorities.

An effective way of forming our sense of identity is with metaphor. A strong metaphor can have an incredible influence on our behaviour by guiding our values and beliefs at both the conscious and unconscious level. Before looking at how we can use the universal alignment model to help our definition of management and leadership, I would like to share some metaphors we consider to be particularly appropriate for leaders.

> A strong metaphor can have an incredible influence on our behaviour by guiding our values and beliefs at both the conscious and unconscious level.

■ The theatre director

You do not see the director during a performance, but you see the results of his work. At rehearsals he is with the actors, encouraging them, giving them feedback, drawing out their personal expression of the characters, and facilitating their stage presence and choreography. The theatre director also works on the group's overall synergy by developing the feeling of complicité, the wider awareness of the other actors' performances. The director knows that a memorable performance requires a strong emotional connection between the actors, the characters they play, and the audience. It is not enough simply to go through the motions. Hearts and minds must be fully engaged to create the energy needed to draw the audience into the performance. And still the director never appears while the curtain is up. He knows that success is defined by the audience, and it is the actors' confidence and ability that, through their energy, make the emotional connection that will lead to a successful performance.

If leaders in your organisation were to model themselves on the metaphor of the theatre director, how might this influence their behaviour?

■ Energy meridians

Chinese medicine identifies a number of meridians in the body connecting the internal organs, and through which vital life energy flows. Good health is the result of smooth energy, or chi, circulation, without deficiency or accumulation. Disease is often associated with blockages in certain meridians restricting the flow of energy. In many ways leaders are the meridians of an organisation, having control over energy, being able to turn it on and off as required, or route it to where it is needed most. In Chinese medicine there is a strong emphasis on preventative health measures, taking a holistic view of the body, the mind and the environment. As a leader, working on the environment to create a healthy climate for people to think and interact, keeping the energy meridians open, and channelling energy to where it is needed, might also be a useful metaphor.

■ Making better ball

It was only after I had been playing rugby for fifteen years or so that I learned the most useful lesson of all. Playing in the position of centre, I am in the middle of a line of five or six players. Our purpose is to run with ball in hand, interpassing or perhaps kicking ahead, to touch the ball down over the opposing team's goal line. As a centre, I have a number of options, I can catch and pass, kick through, deliver a long pass missing one or two players outside me, or make a break by running past the players opposite.

The advice that made a vital difference to my performance was simple. My job is to 'make better ball'. My options remain the same, catching, passing, kicking or breaking, yet now I have a new standard against which to make my decisions – better ball. How can I put the team in an improved position by making better ball? Sometimes, to have better ball, it might be best for me to pick a particular option, or even to allow the ball to travel past me to the next, better positioned player. Everything can be judged by its impact upon the quality of the ball.

The leadership equivalent is powerful indeed to me. Can we consider every interaction by our affect on others? Does one option or another leave people more capable? Perhaps our role as leader is to build up our people with every opportunity we have – to make better people.

■ The midwife

For this metaphor, we have drawn upon John Heider's[3] excellent book *The Tao of Leadership*, which reminds us that an effective leader facilitates processes in much the same way that a midwife facilitates a birth:

> Remember that you are facilitating another person's process. It is not your process. Do not intrude. Do not control. Do not force your own needs and insights into the foreground. If you do not trust a person's process, that person will not trust you. Imagine that you are a midwife; you are assisting at someone else's birth. Do good without show or fuss. Facilitate what is happening, not what you think ought to be happening. If you must take the lead, lead so that the mother is helped, yet still free and in charge. When the baby is born the mother will rightly say: 'We did it ourselves!'

There are many metaphors used by those entrusted with an organisation's resources, and many are disempowering. Certain economic strategies are based on 'running a tight ship', creating a competitive demand for seemingly inadequate resources, requiring managers to squeeze more energy from less substance. 'Drawing blood from a stone' is the ultimate victory in these environments.

One vice-president I was assigned to coach wanted to learn how better to influence people. His performance to date had not been sufficient to distinguish him with the top echelons of the company. We discovered one of the causes in his own personal metaphors taken straight from the military phrasebook. He would talk of his relationship with the board in a variety of ways, as if it were a war, with language such as 'they're out to kill me', 'I'll outflank them', 'I must outmanoeuvre them'. As his coach I suggested he learn to dance instead, suggesting a more empowering metaphor with this very different language. If he could 'pick up the beat', 'get into step with his partner', then we felt a new 'synchronised motion' would develop with a better 'rhythm'. People might even end up on 'the same wavelength'.

Another of my coaching clients wanted to learn how to 'get people to agree with me without using the big guns'. This metaphor was a reflection of his fascination with weaponry, and was totally disempowering for himself and those he worked with. I decided not to allow him into the room unless he metaphorically disarmed himself first. This was the first step to an improved metaphor for persuasion.

> **Whatever the circumstances, a leader is someone who lights the way for others.**

Inner alignment

Whatever the circumstances, a leader is someone who lights the way for others. Whenever we have been privileged to work with effective and respected leaders over the years, we have intentionally modelled the key drivers to their success. Our findings reveal a common inner personal alignment, showing through consistently over time as a well-balanced and congruent sense of self and purpose. The most appropriate leadership action for any situation is more likely to be the

> **The most appropriate leadership action for any situation is more likely to be the result of an inner personal alignment than any textbook technique.**

result of an inner personal alignment than any textbook technique. So, the personal development of leaders might best be facilitated using the alignment model. Let us take a look at the key leadership drivers.

■ Staying true to purpose

This key driver recognises that senses can become drowned in the sea of action, and that connections to aims, outcomes and purpose are easily clouded by the exigencies of the day. Customer needs are continually changing as product and service specifications become more sophisticated. No business can afford to stand still and expect to survive. The purpose of any particular function within an organisation can no longer be taken for granted as it could in the past, things are changing too fast for that. Effective leaders frequently take time out, with others, to calm the senses, reflect on action and make reference to higher levels of purpose and direction. Often purpose will be redefined, and perhaps a new mission statement will be drafted accordingly. This activity is carried out with a dissociation from the action of work, so that rational connections between purpose and action can be defined. During time-out sessions connections along the alignment levels are reformed and strengthened. Mission, goals or outcomes, strategies and actions are all up for reevaluation, and people's hearts and minds are given the opportunity to realign with a revised purpose.

> Effective leaders frequently take time out, with others, to calm the senses, reflect on action and make reference to higher levels of purpose and direction.

■ Positively emphasise 'being' as well as 'doing'

You will hear an effective leader asking questions about identity, not just action. With such a strong emphasis on the detail of activity in organisations the sense of belonging to a unified team can wear thin. To say 'we will all have to work harder and pay attention to the important issues at hand' is a statement of activity. In comparison to ask 'in what way can we become most proficient and successful in this function?' is a question which encourages the creation of a strong identity, and leaves the field open for personal interpretation. It is empowering not stifling, holistic not fragmented, respectful not assuming. Language has an impact on others which can be either empowering or disempowering. If, as leaders, our job is to develop a team's contribution to organisational aims and objectives, we can be most effective at this by encouraging personal and team confidence, thus creating the momentum to increase capability.

At times we may want to give someone some feedback about performance, either in recognition of a job done well, or in response to a less successful endeavour. Here again our language is crucial to the impact on the individual or team. If our outcome is to empower and develop capability, it will be necessary to separate the person from the behaviour. To say 'you're lazy', or 'you lack focus' is disempowering by linking the behaviour to the person's identity. It is much more empowering to feed back behaviour in terms of 'what was done', rather than 'what you are' – to say 'you picked up on the large sums, and excluded some smaller, but important costs', is better than 'you lack concentration and focus'. Generalisations such as this serve to form a weakened sense of identity. There are many feedback loops in organisations, some are often interpreted as assaults on personal effort. Positive encouragement is needed to address the imbalance and to build self-confidence and self-esteem among individuals and teams.

We are reminded of one client's recent sustained period of high growth which created an escalating workload for employees. Many people felt stressed and drained by the increased pressure, but the CEO, recognising the commitment shown by employees, explained how it was like 'riding the tiger' and it seemed to give people a deeper sense of meaning in recognition of their hard work.

■ Talk and embody 'values'

If values are to be of any utility they must find their way into the day-to-day language of employees. The effective leader will draw upon organisational and personal values to help the decision-making process. In this way, the leader is able to role model the use of values for others, demonstrating their function in a variety of contexts. Merely stating a value is insufficient, there must be a consequential link to action: for example, 'To answer your question it is important to recognise the *value* we put on *creativity*, and so I might suggest you spend more time brainstorming to create more options before deciding when you will proceed with this project.' A recent experience showed a management group the folly of its ways when during a workshop it was decided that back-biting among the group should stop. At dinner the same day, however, they continued to assassinate the characters of their absent colleagues. My intervention, reminding them of the value they agreed upon not to do this, encouraged them to find alternative topics of conversation.

> If values are to be of any utility they must find their way into the day-to-day language of employees.

> We need to intervene consciously in established routines, introducing more resourceful alternatives.

Old habits and accustomed ways of thinking rarely change overnight simply because we want them too. We need to intervene consciously in established routines, introducing more resourceful alternatives.

■ Hold empowering beliefs

There are many limiting beliefs held by individuals and teams in organisations. They can include limiting beliefs about possibility, capability, what should or should not be done, rules and expectations. The leader is in a position to challenge limiting beliefs and offer alternatives. Beliefs are incredibly powerful, setting the limits to our capability, and should therefore be treated with great respect.

> Beliefs are incredibly powerful, setting the limits to our capability, and should therefore be treated with great respect.

There is a simple test to ascertain whether a belief is grounded in any substance that may or may not be of use. As you read the following list of beliefs, which can be heard in organisations every day, ask each of the questions in the right-hand column for each belief statement in the left. You might try this with your own statements of belief to experience the true effect of the questions.

Statement of belief	Empowering questions
We can't do that.	What prevents you?
They won't co-operate.	How many different ways have you tried so far?
They're not interested in our ideas.	How could you get them interested?
They'll never change.	Never?
I'm no good at formal presentations.	What evidence do you have? No good compared to whom? Would you like to be good at presentations?
I couldn't do that.	Do you want to? What stops you?
No one will take any notice.	No one at all? In how many ways have you tried to draw attention?
He won't listen to me.	How do you know? Will you listen to him?
We must hit the target.	What will happen if you don't?

The questions in the right-hand column cause the person making the statement to think more carefully about what they are saying, and how they are limiting their flexibility. They are often used in the context of coaching with the purpose of encouraging individuals to generate more options, cover more possibilities and develop their capability. These are all desirable attributes of self-directed and empowered teams. They are empowering in a number of ways:

- The easy way out is no longer an option.
- Limitations are challenged.
- Responsibility remains with the individual.
- The thinking required to take initiative is developed.

So these are the four key drivers which we have modelled from a number of successful and respected leaders in business:

1 Staying true to purpose.
2 Positively emphasise being as well as doing.
3 Talk and embody values.
4 Hold empowering beliefs.

If you were to map these onto the universal alignment model, you would begin to get a picture of how effective leaders harness energy and build commitment in a workforce. None of the key drivers is directly to do with action or capability. Their effect is to ensure that people have a common sense of purpose, a strong sense of identity, empowering beliefs and energising values. It is to this aligning process that the leader's actions are concentrated, language being a precision tool of the trade. The fruits of this aligning process are growing capability and confidence. Action, which is now more a result of individual commitment and team focus, is where the positive results will be recognised.

The leader, through an inner alignment, is a role model enabling others to become aligned with a common cause.

We want to mention two other common aspects of the successful leaders which we have modelled. The first is that they are all lifelong learners, maintaining an intense curiosity to understand how things work so that they can be improved. They do not necessarily invest lots of time in formal learning environments, rather they treat life from waking to sleeping as a continuous learning experience

The second aspect is that they all have a tempered ego, particularly in the company of others. Respect from people around them is created by their general attitude, confidence and ability to create clarity from the confused perceptions of others. This contradicts the idea that effective leaders need to be charismatic. It will surely help but it is not a requirement of success.

As a final metaphor for leadership we draw on the *Tao te Ching*.[4]

The reason why the River and the Sea are able to be King of the hundred valleys is that they excel in taking the lower position ... Therefore, desiring to rule over the people,

One must in one's words humble oneself before them;
And, desiring to lead the people,
One must, in one's person, follow behind them.
Therefore the sage takes his place over the people yet is no burden; takes his place ahead of the people yet causes no obstruction. That is why the empire supports him joyfully and never tires of doing so. It is because he does not contend that no one in the empire is in a position to contend with him.

Personal leadership alignment checklist

Try the following questions, which have been formed to help you explore the alignment distinctions in this context. In each case answer the questions honestly and candidly, the awareness so gained can be a stepping stone to further development.

In what contexts are you a leader?

What is involved in your purpose as a leader?

What is not included in your purpose?

What is your sense of yourself as a leader, in the form of a metaphor?

What kind of leader are you not?

_____

_____

What are your most important values as a leader?

_____

_____

Which of your values could conflict with being a great leader?

_____

_____

What rules and beliefs do you adopt as a leader?

_____

_____

What rules and beliefs are inappropriate in your leadership role?

_____

_____

What potential do you have as a leader?

_____

_____

What potential do you not have?

_____

_____

What do you do as a leader?

_____

_____

What do you not do as a leader?

_____

_____

Notes

1 Michael Simmons (1996) *New Leadership for Women and Men*. Gower.
2 William C Byham and Jeff Cox (1991) *ZAPP: The Lightning of Empowerment*. Century Business.
3 John Heider (1986) *The Tao of Leadership*. Gower.
4 Lao Tzu (1963) *Tao te Ching*. Penguin Classics.

8

TEAM ALIGNMENT

Introduction

In any type of organisation, whether commercial, altruistic or regulatory in nature, the degree of efficiency and effectiveness will be determined, to a great extent, by the way tasks are defined and shared among its members. Most people will have a number of experiences of being a team member, and some understanding of what constitutes a successful team. There is an abundance of material available on this topic, a reflection perhaps of how the team is clearly recognised as the basic unit of organisation in modern work environments. And yet, despite this emphasis on teamworking we continue to hear reports from our clients telling us that there is much to do in helping their teams to achieve consistent high performance. So this is where we shift our focus using the alignment model to determine the key building blocks for high performance teams. We begin with purpose.

> **All too often purpose is not expressly addressed by the team.**

Purpose

A team purpose provides a unifying and motivating reason for everything the team is trying to do. All too often purpose is not expressly addressed by the team. People are then left to toil within a context which they infer and create from what they see around them and from their own thoughts and intentions.

> As a young graduate I worked within parts of ICI where there seemed to be little or no purpose specifically communicated to the production teams. As such, the largest sense of purpose experienced by some of the staff was to meet the attendance criteria necessary to get paid each Thursday.

The absence of an agreed purpose removes the longer term constant of direction that helps set so many short-term situations in a larger context. Those same employees might have been able to act in a different way had they felt connected to the purpose of the group to which they belonged. The purpose could perhaps have been to produce products which were valuable to society and which needed a great deal of care and skill to produce safely. This is clear context which can be deliberately introduced, discussed and understood by all. As such, it would have provided direction in a way which was otherwise completely missing for people.

Purpose is the reason for being. We want to know for what purpose the team has been formed. What is the specific aim of this team? This answer will help to inform the group's thinking on this most central issue. Experience shows that even quite well-developed teams have different interpretations of a purpose if the issue has not been centrally addressed for all to answer.

> **We want to know for what purpose the team has been formed.**

Our plans miscarry because they have no aim. When a man does not know what harbour he is making for, no wind is the right wind. [Seneca]

Results

Performance management systems frequently cover in great detail the contribution that individuals are expected to make to the corporate mission. Less well-covered are the results expected of teams. But, just as you would never dream of sending a team out onto the sports- or battlefield without a clear sense of the collective results needed of it, we need to make sure our teams know what results are required of them in their daily activities. An exercise in communication might be all that is needed, providing that someone, most likely the leader, has already clearly thought through what the targets are. If this is not the case then a great deal of consultation and reflection might be needed to determine what the team will achieve.

Answers to the following questions will ensure a degree of clarity about what exactly the team is doing. The results that are required can be thought of as a set of outputs that will be delivered by the team come what may.

Questions to help a team set its direction:

* What do we need to do in order to achieve our purpose?

  _____

  _____

* What are the ten-year, five-year, two-year, one-year, six-month, three-month and one-month milestones which will allow us to know that we are reaching our goals?

  _____

  _____

* What will be the evidence that we have achieved each of these?

  _____

  _____

* What are the measures we can apply to our output to ensure it is consistently meeting the standard of performance that we judge is acceptable?

  _____

  _____

* How will we know when we are performing above or below this standard?

  _____

  _____

Identity

Can you imagine how it feels to pull on a Manchester United shirt, a Chicago Bulls vest or perhaps an All Black jersey? Sean Fitzpatrick, longest ever serving All Black skipper, tells of how any All

Black will identify with a heritage of more than one hundred years. His team mates do not simply play rugby together, they join and embody a tradition of playing the best rugby in the world. They become All Blacks. The black jersey and the silver fern are the most visible signs of the team identity, but the most significant cohesion exists in the common attitudes expected of every All Black. It is perhaps these attitudes above any other single factor which allow the small nation of New Zealand to have remained at or very near the top of this sport for so many years. The population of around 3 million people regularly produces outstanding players, yet even when the star quotient is below its highest they still turn out great teams.

The team values demand the highest level of commitment, fitness and skill from everyone. The efforts put into practicing together and into reaching high levels of fitness are phenomenal, each player acting in accord with these values. These teams also value playing great rugby, not just winning. Occasionally mismatched with weak opposition in World Cup tournaments, they have proceeded to demolish the unfortunate XV opposite them in a ruthless fashion, using the opportunity to hone their collective skills. The attitude gestalt of All Blacks includes some beliefs that are also incredibly powerful.

First, they believe they will win each and every game, a powerful inner confidence which enables them to take the field with a significant advantage against any opponents who have even the slightest self-doubt. Second, to lose is unthinkable, to lose is to betray the heritage of all those years, to let down the great men of the past who have pulled on the All Black shirt. Translated into action this produces a cool resourcefulness in finding how to overcome tough opponents and win.

Yes, teams have identities, teams need clear identities to work well and in business working at the identity level with teams is often ignored. Who are we? The answers to this one can sit anywhere along a spectrum from All Black cohesion to a near-zero common identity where people simply work in close proximity to others employed by the same organisation. Clear identity is linked very closely to role. The All Black identity is inseparable from their role on a sports field. In organisational life team roles are usually identifiable but not always clearly described. And the difference between these two is often simply that of being explicit. In the absence of discussion about what the team role and

> **In organisational life team roles are usually identifiable but not always clearly described.**

the team identity are each member will give varying amounts of conscious thought to the question and will likely come to different conclusions. Team alignment needs these ideas to be frequently articulated and clarified. By this we do not want to imply that reaching a common identity is always as simple as discussion.

One of the organisations we work with has a small team employed in providing a relocation service to large, mainly multinational organisations, helping those companies in the various activities involved in moving key staff around the world. The team involved originally saw itself as a service provider, focused around helping the people and families who were on the move look for new homes, schools for the kids and the other links that would allow them to recreate a happy home environment. Circumstances now thrust that team much closer to the sharp end of the business, winning new accounts, exploring opportunities for expanding the work done with existing customers, selling itself and doing all of this at an unprecedented level of activity. This team is in the middle of an identity shift. The managers are working hard at different levels to reinforce this shift. Their daily work needs to include not only providing service, but also marketing and development activities. Management interest must be consistently and empathetically shown in the progression from service to service-plus. The team needs to be involved in forming the messages that it will be spreading about its own capability, it needs to have to hand good resources that will help: brochures, a website, databases of information, contacts that can be useful and good, solid procedures. The team needs different capabilities, so training is being provided in various new software packages or in the activities required. And all of this without denting or losing the values that these dedicated people place on professional and flexible service. It is not an overnight process bringing them to identify as a business unit instead of a service team. It might take some months for the shift to complete, during which the managers need to keep patiently moving step by step and reinforcing the new attitudes and behaviours.

Values and beliefs

Teams represent an interesting midpoint between the corporate and the individual, a place where one person's efforts begin to combine with others' to produce results on behalf of the organisation. Nowhere is this more important than in the realm of values and beliefs. Today there are few organisations without some type of statement about values, either expressed directly or inferred in corporate mission statements and visions. Every team within that organisation will be expected to reflect those values in its own activities. Yet for teams to operate more effectively they often need more detailed value statements and rules than those provided by corporate level statements. Locally, teams have the opportunity to add to and embellish the corporate with their own unique interpretation. The team is the context in which corporate values need to be translated into acceptable and unacceptable behaviours for individual employees. This is the level at which rules need to become explicit. This is what brings about the marriage of individual and corporate existence.

The team is the context in which corporate values need to be translated into acceptable and unacceptable behaviours for individual employees.

The challenge is explicitly to agree what is important within the team and the rules that will allow the team to perform. The scope of this agreement takes in the three strands of collective performance:

- individual responsibility
- interresponsibility
- team responsibility.

Individual responsibility covers those things for which each individual person can be held accountable. These will be different for each person reflecting her own role and responsibilities. This responsibility is probably already articulated in the performance management process that you use, the performance objectives that each person has. The key is to make these clear to everyone in the team: 'This is what you can expect of me!'

> **Individual responsibility covers those things for which each individual person can be held accountable.**

Interresponsibility is what each team member will do in support of the others. What happens at the end of the day when one person has finished the day's activities and others still have work that needs to be completed? Can, and should, the responsibility to the team output outweigh the completion of individual tasks? Clearly, there is no answer right for every team and every instance, yet it is worth having some agreement in place in advance of this situation occurring so individuals know what is expected of them, they have a rule against which to decide how best to make decisions and choose their behaviour.

> **Interresponsibility is what each team member will do in support of the others.**

Team responsibility implies the outputs that the team wishes to ensure will always be completed. These might be activities which will be done no matter who is at the point of action at any one time. Imagine a team charged with providing response of some kind to customers: it makes a great deal of sense for the team responsibility to extend to a minimum level of service to be provided throughout the day. Telephones will be answered in three rings, for instance, regardless of who is at hand, and cover will remain, even at the expense of lunch breaks.

> **Team responsibility implies the outputs that the team wishes to ensure will always be completed.**

Our experience of teams shows us that teams exist at one of three places in their thinking about values and rules:

■ Unformed

Values and rules might be assumed or inferred but have never been specifically addressed or uniformly communicated.

■ Formed but unused

The framed list is on the wall. Everyone was sent a summary of the conclusions reached on the team day out when it was discussed, but what do we do now? Few people ever refer to these words which remain in the filing cabinet gathering dust and becoming history.

■ A living standard

Here the thinking is not only shaped and agreed by everyone but is alive and kicking as a benchmark for decisions and choices on an everyday basis. Everyone is empowered and encouraged to refer to the standard in his own performance, and managers have the skills and courage to call the team or individual members to account, for behaviour or attitudes measured against this standard.

> Capability for a team is measured as a combination of the people, the systems and the other resources that together allow that team to realise its purpose.

Capabilities

Capability for a team is measured as a combination of the people, the systems and the other resources that together allow that team to realise its purpose. Determining which capabilities need to be deployed in any team requires reference to all of the other levels of the alignment model. The choice we make in assembling the team's total capabilities will depend upon the purpose that the team decides upon and the environment that we operate in.

Our work with the training team in a large retailer demonstrates this very well. After a period of uncertainty about the strategic direction of the business, the training team was formed as a combination of the regional trainers and the head office team. The demands of the business were intense and the team's manager wanted to ensure it had the development opportunities to equip itself for its role. When we began to examine the needs in more detail it became apparent that the team purpose was insufficiently clear. There were different ideas about what the purpose was and there had not been an occasion to discuss it with everyone. At the same time the environment was extremely confusing, different departments and different store managers calling for different types of service. In the middle of all this we sat trying to examine the capabilities the team needed to meet its purpose. We needed a framework with which each of the team could measure their own capabilities versus the team's requirement.

We defined and agreed a new purpose for the team and began to create a sense of collective identity, by discussion and by metaphor. We listed the towards and away from values which the team was prepared to subscribe to, and detailed the behavioural consequences of each. Only then was it really possible to begin to measure the capability needed in the team and the contribution each individual could make to it.

■ Basic principles of teamworking

This book is not the first, nor will it be the last, to address this age-old question of team performance. Our own view of the answer to this can best be explained by reference to the principles that we espouse as guides for purposeful change. Let us examine some of those we consider to be most important in the specific context of teams.

Those who work in any situation are the most capable of designing the best methods and improvements.

This means that a methodology of team building or team management imposed on a team from outside without reference to the team's composition and circumstances is inevitably faulted. We propose that teams are involved in every stage of designing their make-up and methods.

Individuals and teams have a higher capability than is routinely expressed.

One of the meanings of this is that we should aim to harness and stimulate the contribution of individuals to teams, rather than seeking to limit it to specific roles within the overall activity. While team typing can be a useful method of revealing ways in which people may contribute strongly to teams, it all too often has a limiting effect.

Countless times we have encountered people who identify themselves with particular labels after some well-intentioned assessment exercise. Unfortunately, this identity can persist long after the messages of flexibility and adaptability are lost and it results in fixed roles and limited contribution rather than the original intended outcome. We well remember one dysfunctional senior team being guided by its HR director who explained that the inability to work well as a team was attributable to the fact that there were too many people with the same profile within the team, that is, how could we expect anything but problems? This kind of thinking is ultimately disempowering for both individuals and the team. So, how do we unlock this higher capability within each person, and among the people within the team?

In the first instance we can start by mapping out what each of the team members is good at, what each likes doing and wants to do. These are the directions in which we might expect the energy to flow most fully and most naturally. Let us use this energy as it exists, developing a confluence that moves us towards our desired outputs rather than structuring, damming and diverting the flow. How then does the range of preferred activities compare with the range of required activities? And how can the shortfall be made up? These are questions about the team that are best answered by the team. There is no universal right answer, regardless of what you might have read about or been trained in. However, the team might be able to recognise an answer that is appropriate to it and the particular circumstances. Now, it goes without saying that a high degree of team maturity and well-developed team process are required to enable a team to be analysing how best to fill the capability gaps. Individuals who are protective of their own roles or workloads will not easily expand into the opportunity that these questions offer the group. Some firm leadership may be required in the early stages of team forming.

Too often we see team leaders, keen to help, full of laudable intention, imposing team-building ideas on groups of people. In every case where we have

> It is the process of co-ordination that ensures individual activities build into a meaningful whole.

encountered this, we have noticed some degree of resistance to the imposition and an overall loss of energy. As we pointed out in Chapter 3, dynamic energy is created when needs and desires are satisfied by opportunities. Attempting to force-fit people into a preconceived model is likely to suppress their energy and adversely affect overall performance.

At the team level performance is modified and directed by one other capability that deserves to be separately identified and discussed – co-ordinated action. It is the process of co-ordination that ensures individual activities build into a meaningful whole. It is the process of co-ordination that will regulate and adapt the behaviour of the team. Teams need to have the capability to co-ordinate the activities of the individuals. Without this they are only groups arriving at results as much by accident as by any other means.

In recent years there has been a refinement to the way we think about team co-ordination, the advent of self-direction has opened up a new paradigm in our thinking about co-ordinating the activities of groups. Out goes the old order of structure, rank and leadership by command, to be replaced by choice, flexibility, trust and personal leadership. The old order works by utilising the fall-back position available to leaders in organisations which value status. This fall-back is, 'I am responsible so I will decide the what and the how for my team.' This position is the most inelegant and inflexible and is often used to cover up incompetence or a lack of confidence. Table 8.1 suggests an alternative set of capabilities.

Table 8.1 Co-ordinated team action

Old order	New order
Team co-ordination and workflow is designed by the leader for the team	Team co-ordination and workflow is designed by the team for the team
Leader demands respect and compliance from the team for reasons of status and power	Leader earns respect for delegating responsibility and authority (giving power away)
Response to incorrect action includes cover-up and/or blame apportionment	Response to incorrect action is an open curiosity to learn as individuals and as a team
Leader and/or expert is the font of all knowledge	Leaders and experts are role models for open learning
Leader and/or expert is the source of all major decisions	Leaders and experts are the embodiment of personal empowerment

Team behaviour

From our experience of observing teams we have developed five categories to help understand different levels of team effectiveness, and within these categories we can examine a range of team behaviours using the alignment model to make important distinctions.

■ Crowd

A crowd is the loosest form of group. It has a common environment, having assembled in the same place at the same time, but the behaviour lacks co-ordination. Do not be fooled by any appearance of common behaviour, this is more coincidence and group compliance than co-ordination. There is no choice of membership or deliberate collection of related capabilities. Individuals will share attitudes only to the extent that there is a coincidental overlap.

■ Herd

A herd is a group of individuals which exist together and move together; they do the same things at much the same time and they can even derive benefit from each other. Group members share an environment and exhibit common behaviours, yet they lack the key team capability of co-ordination. A lion will pick off the weakest or youngest wildebeest from the herd. The rest of the herd will exhibit the behaviour of flight but will not have taken any preventative behaviour to stop this happening, and do not demonstrate any co-ordinated response to the threat once it is recognised. There is neither leadership to provide co-ordination nor the capability to self-regulate. They are incapable of developing a direction on their own initiative. The highest level at which a herd can function is to improve their individual or collective environment. At work herds are rare. Almost any kind of leadership can be enough to bring the co-ordination they miss.

■ Swarm

A swarm is a group with a spread of different skills and behaviours at its disposal and with the ability to combine these activities for the collective good. A natural example of this is bees with their ability to combine and communicate well enough to lead the hive of worker bees to pollen, then to act collectively to ferry the pollen back to the hive for the good of all. This behaviour is impressive, but limited to a particular function: pollen collection.

Bees are unable to increase their capability to perform differently outside this scope of activity. In our organisations, this is the well-rehearsed group which goes through practised routines in an efficient way but lacks the cohesion required to make collective decisions when faced with changing circumstances. Shared purpose and shared values would provide this and would allow it to analyse problems and to choose how best to adapt to the changes around it or shape the environment to better suit its purpose.

■ Team

A team works to a higher degree of flexibility. It is an assembly of different talents, with shared values and agreed rules of co-operation. Think about the international alliances formed to meet perceived threats to world order. The United Nations task forces represent the best of the capability of different nations, combined in a military style of communication and co-ordination. The alliance sets off with explicitly shared values and a common aim. What limits the performance of the alliance is the lack of a common understanding of identity. Perhaps the blue beret simply is not enough of an identity to knit together the different nationalities over a sustained period of high intensity activity.

■ Cast

This is the cast of a theatre company chosen for its ability to overlap all of the alignment distinctions, starting with a common purpose, an established and strong identity with values and beliefs or rules attached to that identity. Thereafter, a cast has the capability to co-ordinate extremely well and the behaviour or performance that transpires is more flexible, appropriate and effective in a wider range of contexts than it is for teams, swarms, herds and crowds.

A cast has a great deal to offer the workteam with many parallels to be drawn. For instance, a cast comes together for a specific performance. Actors are selected for experience and ability to take on the personas of particular characters, before the lengthy, often arduous but developmental stage of rehearsal. Personal expression and interpretation become part of the characters, producing a uniquely branded performance. The environment in which a cast will perform is the theatre, or as the world-famous director, Peter Brook,[1] would have it 'an empty space' where anything could and does happen. There is a clear purpose to entertain; a strong identity with the characters and the setting of the play; artistic interpretation features highly among professional casts, as does teamworking, which is often referred to as complicité or being an accomplice. The theatre translation of this is to have an awareness, through all senses, of what others are doing even when you are playing your part. Others in this case includes the audience. Without this no amount of creative genius can succeed. A cast needs the capability to play parts across a wide emotional range, and behavioural flexibility ranging from Greek tragedy to satirical comedy. Whatever the production, the cast is able to bring collective experience and capability to meet the need. If a team were to organise itself as a cast, think how it might focus the attention. What might rehearsals be like? How would complicité be achieved? What values might the team choose for its unique interpretation of the work?

■ Team questionnaire

Answer the following questions, awarding yourself the score which most closely matches the situation in your team:

	Poor/never			Very good/always	
	0	1	2	3	4	5

1 How often do you see one another?

| 0 | 1 | 2 | 3 | 4 | 5 |

2 Do you hold team meetings: weekly – 5, monthly – 3, occasionally – 1?

| 0 | 1 | 2 | 3 | 4 | 5 |

3 Do team members help one another out with individual workloads?

| 0 | 1 | 2 | 3 | 4 | 5 |

4 To what degree is the team involved in allocating work?

| | 0 | 1 | 2 | 3 | 4 | 5 |

5 Are there clear team targets?

| | 0 | 1 | 2 | 3 | 4 | 5 |

6 Is there a clear team purpose?

| | 0 | 1 | 2 | 3 | 4 | 5 |

7 Have you established a set of values for the team?

| | 0 | 1 | 2 | 3 | 4 | 5 |

8 To what extent do you work together systematically to improve the way in which you carry out the work you do?

| | 0 | 1 | 2 | 3 | 4 | 5 |

9 To what extent do you work together systematically to improve the way in which you work together as a team?

| | 0 | 1 | 2 | 3 | 4 | 5 |

10 Are you able to extend or shape the role of the team within the organisation?

| | 0 | 1 | 2 | 3 | 4 | 5 |

Scoring

0 – 15   This is a crowd. Plenty of work to do.

16 – 28   A herd. Some signs of co-operation but much more needed.

29 – 37   A swarm. This approach is more systematic, yet still has room for improvement.

38 – 44   A team. A good place to be, yet there is a higher level of possibility too.

45 – 50   Congratulations. You are working as a cast, a very high level of co- operation.

Team development

The environment in which organisations are now asking their teams to perform is difficult and infinitely more complex than at any period in the history of organised labour. The pressures on organisations to respond quickly to external threats are high indeed. Global competition raises the stakes considerably, companies now employ far fewer people to run their activities than was ever thought credible. We know of operations in manufacturing, in administration and in service, where less than one-third of the people are now employed to maintain the same scale of activity. How do we set about building teams capable of achieving demanding levels of performance in extreme circumstances such as these? To begin to answer this question let us explore dysfunction and its causes.

■ The symptoms

Disease is a word often used as a metaphor for a spreading dysfunction. When you examine diseased teams you find much disease among individuals where their energy is being dissipated and not utilised for the common good of the team, the company, its stakeholders and all the other employees. Table 8.2 shows some of the most common symptoms from our experience. They are based on the simple fact that people bring their energy to work and decide how to burn it based on personal interpretations of their relationship with other employees and the culture.

Table 8.2 Dis-ease and teams

DIS-EASED TEAMS OFTEN USE THEIR ENERGY INAPPROPRIATELY

Complying to commands	rather than ...	being curious to learn better ways
Attention outside the organisation for career prospects	and little ...	expectation of advancement within the organisation
Networking outside the organisation for personal gain	rather than ...	developing contacts to help the team from inside and outside the organisation
Protecting self and team from salvos of blame, often apportioning blame elsewhere	instead of ...	learning from others and developing co-operative links with other teams
Keeping information and technical knowledge securely locked away	instead of ...	developing free, open access to their knowledge base for wider use in the organisation
Spending much time persuading reluctant others to participate in projects	rather than ...	cross-team project meetings being an important and enjoyable part of everyday work
Negative feelings created from a poor reputation in the wider community caused by incongruence (say one thing, do another)	and not ...	feeling good from experiencing on a daily basis the company's espoused mission, values and beliefs

■ Common causes

There are many causes for dis-ease in teams, and the alignment principle helps to identify the most common and most cancerous. However, our purpose in this chapter is to suggest what to do, rather than what to avoid.

Invisible purpose

Purpose needs to be clear to all and adopted by all. If either of these criteria is not met the efforts of the team may be undermined. Making purpose clear is one of the key leadership roles. This is sometimes described as providing vision. Purpose is related to vision and effective leadership will ensure both are revealed. The key to the second part of this is to ensure commitment to the vision and the purpose across the whole team.

> Making purpose clear is one of the key leadership roles.

This should never be assumed, since, even with the most articulate of speeches, understanding and personal connection with your purpose may be less than desired. To gain commitment, it is necessary for individuals to interpret the purpose for themselves, to have the opportunity to determine how their work will be organised to fulfil the purpose best. The

> Commitment to one's own ideas, or the collective ideas of your team, is always stronger than to the ideas imposed by others.

leader's role here is to encourage a culture of involvement where individuals have a say in designing their environment. This is a very basic human principle. Commitment to one's own ideas, or the collective ideas of your team, is always stronger than to the ideas imposed by others.

Many years ago, my own team of computer analysts was searching for a higher purpose. We had developed our services to an effective level and were getting regular praise from our internal clients. I knew that the most senior members needed stretching, but found it difficult to address these needs within the organisation. This shouldn't have been the case. There were areas in the company where they could contribute and develop, but at the time the general managers were at war. The effect of this was to create a void between operating divisions where the higher purpose became very foggy. People retracted into their own isolated worlds, not wanting to be con taminated by the dis-ease. Eventually, we looked outside the organisation and it is pleasing to know that every member of that team went on to develop her potential and we remain very close friends today.

Identity crisis

'I realise now that for the past three years I have been doing my bosses' dirty work. Since meeting other people from different organisations I realise that the company I work for is only interested in what it can get from people. We are all working flat out doing in excess of a 12-hour day, often without lunch breaks. I have fired people because they couldn't do their job to specific standards. The management methods in my company are archaic to say the least. Well, I'm going to be different from now on. I'm going to make an effort to understand, work with and develop my people, and if that doesn't fit the culture I will gladly leave. In fact, like most people in this company, I scan the job ads every day looking for an escape route.'

This was the changing identity of a senior manager after a day on one of our open management programmes, paid for by her company. We do not know what they expected, but they will have to live with the consequences of the identity change. For years she had tolerated an identity crisis, knowing deep inside, at an emotional level, that the effect of the company's management style was dehumanising, but for personal reasons she chose to live with it before resolving the internal crisis which grew stronger day by day.

Values mismatch

The management development manager had been working really hard to support the pace of change during a key time within his company. What was beginning to trouble him was the way in which decisions were being made about other managers. Data gathered at development centres were being used to make judgements about who to retain and who to make redundant as the company slimmed down its UK operations. This just didn't seem right. The managers involved had been participating in the belief that they were there to develop their own capabilities. There had been no mention of assessment, which he viewed as a very different process. That wasn't all, there were other signs emerging that senior managers were not respecting the pressures and uncertainties that the organisation had been going through. At least, that was his view. And in a coaching session he revealed how deeply this was affecting him.

When we perceive that our own deeply held values are being ignored or infringed on it sets up an internal tension. Often this can be ignored, played down or rationalised. It is a question of degree. In this case, the reaction of the individual was approaching critical, he knew in his heart that he could no longer apply himself totally to that organisation. When individuals begin to form values that go against those of their organisation, a cancer takes root and spreads silently. It becomes apparent when key people leave in numbers, and the ensuing action required to

> **When we perceive that our own deeply held values are being ignored or infringed on it sets up an internal tension.**

eradicate the cancer is very extensive and costly to the organisation.

Values interpretation

> *'I remember the sense of outrage very well. They told me that they valued me, they thought I was making good progress in the company, and that they thought I was capable of assuming this new level of responsibility, that it was an important and exposed role. Oh, and by the way we aren't prepared to pay you the full grade for the job because of your youth, please make do on a lower grade.'*

This is a quote from one of our coaching clients. She left that company to work for another which demonstrated her value to them by way of increased responsibility, development opportunities and remuneration. Values can be expressed in a number of ways, one is the spoken word. Yet it is the way in which we interpret our values in action which provides the real evidence of whether we are true to the values we espouse.

Capability mix

> *'It wasn't a lack of willingness in any of the individuals involved. That seemed pretty clear. They simply didn't have the rapid facility they needed to develop high quality output.'*

This is another quote from one of our clients who was referring to a team of customer service engineers. The company was reluctant to invest in the infrastructure to support the team's efforts. Training, materials, test equipment and communication devices were far less than adequate. Access to technical support information was also blocked, not intentionally, rather through neglect. So not only was the team held back by the lack of investment, nowhere in the planning process was there any mention of 'developing future capability', and this had an adverse impact on customers. Although the team consisted of highly capable individuals, the capability as a team was inhibited by lack of resources.

A team may be fully aligned with the organisation's purpose, and yet be restricted by misalignments elsewhere in the company. Access to vital resources must be attended to, the people responsible ensuring that their sense of priorities is synchronised with the people who need the resources. A poor capability mix is often a sign of conflicting priorities and mixed purposes. Teams will endure this for so long, relying on their professionalism to stay committed to customers, until they reach breaking point. Thereafter, turning on the resource tap is not enough. Trust must be rebuilt and respect earned. This can take some time.

Co-ordination

> 'It's a matter of yards from the plant to the office where the sales administration staff sit. Yet despite this there are daily wrangles about what should be produced next on the order plan and what should be shipped off to stock or to particular customers. The office team don't know any of the production staff. The production team don't feel welcome in the office and all of the communication is between the two team leaders. Time and efficiency are surrendered in this confusion.'

No matter how well-organised any particular team is, its overall effectiveness will depend on co-ordination with other teams and resources in the organisation. In an orchestra, the most polished string section will not add to the listeners' enjoyment of the music unless it is well co-ordinated with all of the other sections. To accomplish this, each section of the orchestra can see the entire orchestral score and acts as directed by the conductor. This delivers the necessary degree of synchronisation and a common interpretation of the overall piece.

In organisational terms, the music score and the conductor are not always so apparent.

The numbers problem

'It's an uphill task, every day, just to keep up with the work coming in. I'm worried we'll miss something. I haven't got time to write out the invoices for what we've done, and I'm sorry but there's no chance of me doing the monthly report.'

So said one of the managers who worked with me as her small team struggled under a surge in the order book. How can you tell if there are insufficient people on the team if you have not tried to resolve all of the other possible problems? A growing organisation will need to recruit people, that is a given, but how many people? And how can you be sure that existing people are working in the smartest way possible, and that work is organised to optimum effect? The answer is by integrating the alignment model into the team process using a set of key principles applied rigorously on a daily basis.

A principled approach to better teamwork

There are perhaps two key elements involved in improving teamwork which hinge on open communication and a degree of maturity.

Teams need explicitly to discuss the alignment distinctions.

Opportunities need to be fashioned for debate about team purpose, results, attitudes, capabilities and the desired action. Done openly, a clarity will emerge making misunderstanding and conflict less likely. And in the event that problems do emerge, there is a reference point already agreed against which individual decisions and behaviours can be evaluated.

The second key is for teams to learn how to bring issues of any kind to the surface and to discuss them openly and honestly.

Almost any issues can be resolved by mature discussion, particularly when there is a pre-agreed framework of values and purpose.

These words are easily written, yet we recognise that they require a great deal of skill, patience and energy to bring into reality. The reason so many teams fall short of the ideal of openness is not because people do not know that it is important. We know from our own personal experience it is no lack of desire, it is just so often easier not to raise an issue, not to rock the boat and to settle for a sub-optimal situation rather than pursue the ideal. Or it could be that these critical factors of team performance are not associated with the prevailing everyday business dialogue and so people keep their feelings to themselves.

The following set of principles will guide a group of people in the direction needed to become a cast.

■ Team alignment principles

1 Encourage a high degree of team involvement in decisions about the design and implementation of the team's work and working conditions.

2 Integrate learning into work processes. Make learning a part of the work, not a separate activity.

3 Seek to increase the level of responsibility and authority for individuals, enabling them to achieve more. Team leaders should seek to give away their power in an organised and aligned way.

4 Team members should be encouraged to develop personal leadership qualities to help their ongoing development and the team's overall capability.

5 Dialogues about each of the distinctions of the alignment model should be frequent. These dialogues should be used at formal meetings, and informally, to help make day-to-day decisions. Through dialogue we can learn from our experience and move on to greater things.

In the last ten years we have encountered a completely new paradigm, that of self-direction for teams. This has spawned many different initiatives in different organisations, but whatever form they take they are tapping into a basic principle that teams are capable of organising themselves, and are not in need of direction from managers or leaders in a way which was once assumed to be necessary. Whether you approach teamworking as one of the team, as a team leader or as a consultant or other third party observer, the principle of alignment will help you to steer a worthwhile course.

Note

1 Peter Brook (1990) *The Empty Space*. Penguin.

9

INNOVATION

Introduction

Another way in which organisations are aiming to react to their environment is through innovation. As a strategy this holds out the promise of great success. We conjure up thoughts of a stream of new products or services drawing customers away from our competitors. We can envisage a range of improvements to the processes that currently underpin our business reducing congestion or confusion and slashing costs. No surprise then that companies large and small are showing a renewed interest in the topic.

What is innovation?

Peter Brabecke, CEO of Nestlé, declared in 1997 that renovation and innovation would be two of the four pillars of this giant's strategy through the early years of the new millennium. His company has turned to ours for ideas. How can we use the concept of alignment to develop our understanding of how innovation can be supported, or suppressed, in this or any other company?

> We define innovation as the successful exploitation of new ideas.

As we saw with leadership, there is a strong action element to innovation. If an organisation can be doing the right things then innovation occurs. Yet the understanding of what is involved is often limited. We revel in our mystification of these processes. There are at least two UK advertising campaigns we can recall which play on the image of boffin-type research scientists. White-coated and toting clipboards, they are engaged in various technical activities apparently leading to some product breakthrough of particular benefit to the consumer. Once again, mankind is indebted to impenetrable science for its day-to-day quality of life.

In reality, innovation is a very accessible process, not involving technicians in many instances. We define innovation as the successful exploitation of new ideas. This tells us straight away that it can happen as easily in a catering company or the money markets as a high-tech pharmaceutical laboratory. It can involve new products, but is just as likely to focus on improving the production or distribution of well-established products. And it is as relevant to service industries as it is to manufacturers.

Alongside the activities of innovation sit the attitudes of innovation. Once again the parallel with leadership is interesting. Once again it is most often the attitudes in organisations that most significantly inhibit the birth and exploitation of new ideas. Several examples come to mind of the different ways in which organisations discourage by deed at the same time as they encourage by word.

I recall managers in another food company telling me about their attempts to pilot a new range of pre-prepared meals in a new category of the market. They had spotted the trend toward more health-conscious consumption which they wished to exploit and they had developed some products which met the perceived need. They chose a particular country in which they could hold trials and measure the success of their new ideas. Unfortunately, the initial response was poor, partly due to product positioning, labelling and design. It also seemed that customers were not necessarily prepared to support their interest in improved health and well-being if it meant spending more, despite having talked about its importance in all the early market research.

The company's response to this poor initial feedback was telling. The exercise was labelled a failure rather than being considered an incomplete experiment and the marketing team was told to stop all activities forthwith. Such was the culture in that organisation that reputations were almost certainly permanently tarnished and promising careers were slowed down. Most damaging of all was probably the message, carried to every corner of the group by the executive grapevine, 'You can't afford to get it wrong in this company.' Just imagine the impact of that belief. It is impossible to measure the opportunity cost lost by that incident. And, in the meantime, their competitors stayed in the market, adapted their offer, learned a lot more about what would unlock the spending of diet-conscious consumers and stole a march of several years' development on the company.

Contrast this with the story from another company.

When Niall Fitzgerald was being tipped as successor for the post of chief of Unilever, someone recalled how he had been involved in the Persil Power episode. This was an attempt by Unilever to break the stalemate in the soap powder wars by launching a new product, of that name, which was credited with vastly superior performance. Consumers would be unable to resist the step-change in washing effect, and sales, market share and profits would follow.

Unfortunately for Unilever, arch-rivals Procter & Gamble learned that repeated use of the new powder seemed to cause rotting of some fabrics. With some adroit use of PR the message was conveyed quickly to the public, sales of Persil Power failed to materialise, the product was pulled and Unilever was forced to admit a costly mistake. How, it was asked, could the man who presided over the waste of £350m and a humiliating loss of face for the company possibly be promoted to the top slot? The answer came back that as Unilever had just spent £350m educating him it had no choice but to make him CEO.

This story may be true or it may be apocryphal. What is interesting to consider is how much more willing people are to try out new ideas in a company which can learn from mistakes and move on. They have no fear for their position or their career to hold them back. In this way, one of the potential dissuaders of experimentation is removed. The first lesson that needs to be absorbed is how to identify and remove the blocks to innovation.

> **The first lesson that needs to be absorbed is how to identify and remove the blocks to innovation.**

The second lesson is even more powerful, it is how to encourage active innovation. How can we deliberately create the circumstances and activities in which innovation will flourish? Companies need to be able to absorb both of these two lessons. Attention is frequently put into encouraging innovation

> **The second lesson is how to encourage active innovation.**

without first removing the impediments that exist, camouflaged in some way, within the thinking and operating routines that surround our well-intentioned executives. Clearly, such efforts are, at worst, doomed and, at best, undermined from the outset. No stimulation of innovation can be truly effective without weeding out disincentives beforehand. The universal alignment model can offer us a great deal of insight into both of these necessary processes.

The process of innovation

In order to understand the processes of unblocking and of encouraging innovation we need to examine the beast itself. In so doing we find four key elements; Figure 9.1 shows us how they interrelate.

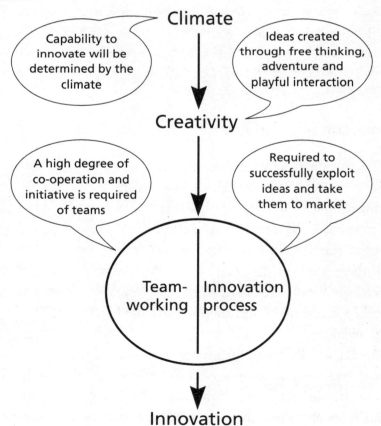

Figure 9.1
The four key elements of innovation

■ Climate

Ideas belong to people, and the degree by which they will readily contribute their ideas depends upon the culture of the organisation and the work group. So the first step is to create a climate of encouragement in which people feel safe innovating, and then beyond that for them to feel positively motivated to get on and do it. This requires that a particular environment is created in which they can work freely. The dimensions of this include the corporate culture which will embody risk taking, difference and challenge – norms that managers must champion.

The business environment will have an impact, too, the mobile communications market will demand more innovation from players in that market than the pseudomarket in which a government revenue collection department exists, for instance. The goals set by the company strategy are another important part of the climate, and let us consider, too, the experience and expectations of the team itself. Getting the climate right is vital, getting it wrong is all too easy, as we shall see.

■ Personal creativity

The next centre for our attention is the individuals involved. Within a supportive environment we can reasonably expect that individuals will begin to deploy their own creativity. For people to do this most effectively they need to know some simple techniques of thinking which can very rapidly raise their creative output. More important is to help individuals to access the natural creativity that we all have, which has lain dormant perhaps for many years, or which was systematically suppressed in our education process. The former requires some development input, the latter calls for more unblocking.

■ Teamworking

Having creative people in a conducive climate gets us about halfway to our goal. Without the capability to combine effectively in teams, however, their individual brilliance can be underutilised. There are particular patterns of interaction which can unlock creative co-operation, and others that will kill it stone dead. Without paying attention to the processes and attitudes at play here, teams will likely remain groups of frustrated individuals. One plus one can sometimes produce only one and three-quarters where collaboration is at a minimum, or it can give us three when individuals' efforts are optimally combined.

■ Systematic implementation

Our last step is to have an accepted, specialised project methodology with which to guide all our new ideas forward. In crude terms this is the difference between invention and innovation.

> **Good ideas are worth nothing until they can be realised.**

Good ideas are worth nothing until they can be realised. Whether this is the introduction of a new product to market or the use of some improvements to an existing process, we need a systematic approach to planning and implementation. Our purpose, therefore, is to beat the odds that otherwise allow new ideas to wither, die or disappear before they reach the stage of commercial success.

■ Innovation questionnaire

Please score your response to each question on the scale provided.

	No/not at all	Some	Yes/highly
	0 1 2 3	4 5 6	7 8 9 10

Climate

1 How important are the processes of change and innovation for your organisation?

0 1 2 3 4 5 6 7 8 9 10

2 Is everyone aware of the purpose of the organisation?

0 1 2 3 4 5 6 7 8 9 10

3 To what extent do you involve everyone in the formation of new ideas and initiatives?

0 1 2 3 4 5 6 7 8 9 10

4 How does your organisation value difference and change?

0 1 2 3 4 5 6 7 8 9 10

Creativity

5 Is creativity apparent in your people and your organisation?

0 1 2 3 4 5 6 7 8 9 10

6 How well-trained are your people in thinking creatively?

0 1 2 3 4 5 6 7 8 9 10

7 Is creativity respected in your organisation?

0 1 2 3 4 5 6 7 8 9 10

8 How well do your working methods encourage the deliberate use of creative thinking by teams?

0 1 2 3 4 5 6 7 8 9 10

Teamworking

9 To what extent do you operate in multifunctional teams?

0 1 2 3 4 5 6 7 8 9 10

10 Are your people trained in teamworking?

0 1 2 3 4 5 6 7 8 9 10

11 Is there a high level of co-operation between teams?

0 1 2 3 4 5 6 7 8 9 10

12 Do teams spend time reviewing their own performance as a team?

0 1 2 3 4 5 6 7 8 9 10

Innovation process

13 Do you have an established methodology for guiding innovation projects to success?

0 1 2 3 4 5 6 7 8 9 10

14 Are your relevant employees trained in a methodology for managing projects?

0 1 2 3 4 5 6 7 8 9 10

15 Do you monitor the ongoing progress of innovation projects in an organised way?

0 1 2 3 4 5 6 7 8 9 10

16 At the end of the project, do you consciously review and learn from the success, or otherwise, of each project?

0 1 2 3 4 5 6 7 8 9 10

Scoring

Add up your scores from the relevant sections and use the table to establish your score as a total (out of a maximum 40 points).

	Questions	Total score
Culture	1, 2, 3, 4	
Creativity	5, 6, 7, 8	
Teamworking	9, 10 , 11, 12	
Innovation process	13, 14, 15, 16	

Aligning for innovation

Attention to the four key elements will expose areas which will require intervention in any organisation. There will be disabling factors to be stripped out and enabling factors to be nurtured. For this, we turn to the alignment model to get a more concentrated focus on some of the things that will require our attention.

> Clearly expressed, a statement of purpose can lead a whole group together to a common destiny.

■ Purpose for innovation

We know that purpose is the most profound expression of what we are trying to do, either as individuals or as organisations. Clearly expressed, a statement of purpose can lead a whole group together to a common destiny. It has the effect of focusing the group's attention on particular outcomes or objectives, and prevents energy being dissipated in blind digressions. Yet in one regard it is like the way in which a flighty racehorse can be concentrated by the application of blinkers. We mask all of the distractions from sight allowing the horse to focus on a much narrower band of vision. In order to get the horse to focus on the track ahead, we are prepared to allow other things to remain out of sight. In a parallel process, when organisations focus hard on particular directions, their purpose, they can lose sight of many other options.

The wave of mega-mergers, in pharmaceuticals, defence, the motor industry and banking, is presumably the culmination of much effort deployed to take those organisations closer to their purpose. In many cases, this will be through maximising returns to shareholders, which for many companies will be central to their purpose. It is also true that all of this activity is, at one level, little more than a rearrangement of the ownership of productive, or unproductive, assets. All of the energy deployed in making the mergers work is energy that cannot be spent on improving the productivity of the assets, save in the crudest way, by cost cutting.

If the same energy were deployed by all levels of the company on improving the product portfolio, the service quality or the effectiveness of current methods, then innovation would be a higher priority in the thinking of all. We know that purpose dictates where energy will flow, and it will also dictate where energy will not flow. Purpose should be chosen with reference to what it excludes as well as sight of what it includes and will deliver. And it is well worth recognising where cross purposes exist – the energy used to pursue one purpose can cancel out the other, resulting in inertia. Think of the effort that gets consumed in the cross purposes of control and empowerment, freedom of expression and conformity, constraint and opportunity. Often an organisation's intended purpose: perhaps 'to deliver value through a motivated and committed workforce' is at odds with what people are really pursuing because of well-rooted unconscious purposes, such as 'efficient operation' or some financial ratio working in opposition to the higher level purpose.

So, when deciding the higher purpose of the organisation, it is also important to consider the wider consequences of pursuing it, and to weed out historically rooted purposes which may exist in the darkest corners of people's unconscious minds.

Make your work to be in keeping with your purpose. [Leonardo da Vinci]

■ Values and beliefs of innovation

When I first set up a training and development consultancy in the early 1990s, I had only limited experience of the activities I would need to offer. What I did know was that there was already no shortage of choice for buyers in this market. The recession and accompanying pruning of executive ranks in the UK had done much to boost the numbers of self-employed consultants plying their trade. Entry costs were low and returns for the single operator with minimal overheads could be more than satisfactory. It was, and remains, a competitive market.

I decided that the only way in which I could compete with the existing providers was to differentiate myself, this meant that I would offer innovative development solutions. This strategy rapidly proved itself successful, and its importance cannot be understated. So completely did I depend on this value to maintain my own confidence to operate that I looked at every single possibility through the lens of the innovator. This didn't mean that everything I did was at the cutting edge of human resource development, indeed I became convinced that innovation was for me relative to the norms already established in the companies who hired my services. In some places, I'm sure that a trainer who smiled seemed innovative. But innovation was lodged so firmly in my mind that I permanently demanded it of myself and my colleagues.

Innovation was an end value for me in those days, I existed to innovate and could only exist (commercially) by innovating. This is the effect that perhaps, in part, accounts for the success of 3M, a company whose very name is synonymous with innovation. If its mentality is still that it exists to innovate then it surely will. In contrast, innovation valued only as a means to an end, rather than as an end in itself, will never be such a motivating force.

What about the other values that impact on the willingness of organisations to tolerate innovation? Innovation always brings uncertainty, risk and difference into play. They are travelling companions. Yet business, and other forms of organised labour, have invested highly to reduce the incidence of these unpredictable elements.

Uncertainty is a given. In business it is accepted that all activity involves risk. We exist within an economic system that allows reward for risk takers by allowing them to retain the profits of their ventures. Yet, outside the ranks of business owners and entrepreneurs, business is populated by those who are best served by the eradication of risk. Anyone employed to manage within an organisation is going to find this role most easily accomplished by the reduction, wherever possible, of risk and uncertainty. Complex operations can be well-planned, and executed to plan most easily, if we can manage uncertainty out of the equation. Money is attracted most readily to a guaranteed return, and the cost of finance rises with the degree of uncertainty. Winning capital support from within the organisation or from outside depends on how certain we can be about a pay-back. In this light, innovation can seem to those who have no experience to the contrary to be something of a lottery. To allow, and to fund, projects which have what appears to be a relatively high chance of failing is a difficult adjustment to make.

> **Innovation always brings uncertainty, risk and difference into play.**

Innovation demands difference, organisation needs conformity. Cross purposes prevail. Who wins? The larger an organisation grows, the more likely it is to exhibit signs of tight control over its workforce. Rules, guidelines and codes of conduct are the formal channels through which this control is exerted. The culture is the informal method to tell people how to behave, what to do and equally, how not to behave and what not to do. And no surprise some organisations have a cloning effect by a combination of their recruitment processes and the formal and informal conforming that follows. IBM's famous dress code was one example of the demand for compliance: Big Blue meant blue suit and white shirt for legions of its male employees.

Yet innovation means going counter-trend, acknowledging what is happening around, yet seeking advantage by doing differently, exploring the opportunities that can be gained by going against the grain. Successful innovation to some degree needs its practitioners to challenge the norm and test the status quo. It takes a brave man or woman to do this when they see conformity being rewarded with the move, the promotion or the pay rise.

Innovation requires risk, which means that some projects will fail, there will be errors of judgement and mistakes along the way. The late Sam Koechlin, CEO of Ciba-Geigy, as was, is reported to have said that he would have loved his managers to come to him each year to tell him of the mistakes they had made. This would have demonstrated that they were trying new things. He recognised that the culture in that company, reinforced as it was by the Swiss culture would not yet encourage this behaviour. At Motorola the motto is, 'We celebrate noble failure.' And yet where we prize accuracy this celebration of mistakes goes against a lifetime's business training.

So, what are the other values that we would wish to propagate in order to support and encourage creativity and innovative behaviour in any group of people, be it an organisation large or small, in business or elsewhere? We could list a few just to start with: learning, creating options, curiosity and experimentation. Perhaps you can think of others. With each of these we again need to explore whether our groups are blocked, knowingly or unknowingly, from working towards these values. And then we need to build these values into the climate in which they operate.

Pick one of these values, learning, for instance. What are the behaviours that go with this value?

- What would someone who valued learning do, or not do?

  _____

  _____

- How does your organisation react towards people doing these things?

  _____

  _____

- How does the performance management system recognise this behaviour?

  _____

  _____

- Are these the actions of the mainstream or the wacky backroom staff?

  _____

  _____

- Would someone be admired or derided for these activities?

  _____

  _____

- Is someone doing this hindering their chance of promotion?

  _____

  _____

Many blockages can be recognised through the following statements and questions, most of which are often held as silent beliefs among people for whom innovation has never before appeared on the menu, or has been discriminated against in the past:

- Why should I innovate? What's in it for me? It means I have to think more, and what will I get in return for this extra thinking?
- No one will listen to my ideas anyway.
- My ideas are not very good.

- No one has appreciated my ideas before, so why should it be any different now?
- Even if I did have an idea it wouldn't be used.

A common response to these frames of mind is to challenge and disagree, stating how it will be different now that innovation really is important. The annual conference is often the vehicle used. This is seldom the most effective way of doing this. A more elegant, congruent and complete method is to work with people within their workteams and help them create their own value for innovation, to facilitate the breaking down of their rigid, silent beliefs so they can build new empowering beliefs which will eventually commit them to innovation.

> **We believe that everyone has the potential to be creative.**

This is the route of exploration we need to tread to see how our organisations really allow innovation-value behaviour.

■ Creative identity

Creativity is an interesting topic, and one which raises strong feelings for some. We believe that everyone has the potential to be creative. That is a statement about human capability, and the innate potential of our species. Sadly, as adults it is not true that we all are creative, either at the level of what we do (action) or the level of how we regard our own abilities (identity).

The conditioning processes of growing up do so much damage to the fragile confidence required in many creative endeavours that we can end up concluding about ourselves that 'I'm not one of those creative types.' Again, this is from personal experience, but we know there will have been a host of similar experiences in classrooms around the world, because every time we recount this story people tell us their versions of the same process.

As a rule, indeed, grown-up people are fairly correct on matters of fact; it is in the higher gift of imagination that they are so sadly to seek.
[Kenneth Grahame]

At my school it was impossible to continue to study all subjects beyond the third year, i.e. age 14. Options needed to be narrowed, exam subjects chosen and some permutations just weren't possible. I was considering the choice of continuing with art and history or studying all of the sciences with double rations of maths. My form teacher was trying to help me to make up my mind, and was, I'm sure, only trying to be helpful when he told me to opt for the latter on the basis that 'You're not really very artistic, Jon.' This was an identity-level statement that allowed little scope for doubt or reevaluation, unalterable it seemed. Was this statement enough on its own to rob me of a sense of my creativity? Certainly not. Yet, coming as it did from an authority figure, it registers in my mind as an important part of shaping my teenage thoughts about myself. And it perhaps indicates, too, how careless and ill-considered words can unintentionally condition the thinking of young and impressionable minds.

Sadly, this experience is all too common and important work often needs to be done with adults to help them overcome the inhibitions that cloak our natural creativity. Some of the factors present in creative activities in school can also be present in the workplace. Comparison, judgement and criticism are each processes that frighten that shy creature, creativity, underground.

> Comparison, judgement and criticism are each processes that frighten that shy creature, creativity, underground.

Repeated, systematised and reinforced in the culture of the company they are likely to make sure that it never tries to emerge again, except in our own time and space, safe from threat and under tight control.

In recent years it has been our objective to increase our own creativity, a goal not unrelated to the business drive of innovation that we referred to earlier. To set up a more creative sense of identity has been central to the expression of our endeavours. This journey has brought us to meet people with similar minds, and together we enrich one another's creative ability. The result is a creative maelstrom of ideas and a further two outcomes: first, we thoroughly enjoy our work, particularly where we can collaborate with one another; second, our client partners gain access to many new and effective ways of developing their business. And herein lies another paradox. We like being asked for ideas which we give freely. We hold a belief that ultimate creativity requires the free use of ideas, and the more of our ideas we can part with, the more we are urged to create new ones. Generating new ideas is something we do all the time. Among our clients there is sometimes a different view, that they want fresh ideas, but only those that have been tried and tested elsewhere. This is different, but low risk, and it does not engage the client in the creative process. At best it will increase their choice of options. Gently, gently, beliefs change and paradigms shift.

Roger van Oech[1] identifies some mental locks which need to be undone in order to stimulate creativity. For example, creativity can be associated with play and frivolity, and this might not fit the particular corporate veneer some people create for organisational life. Creativity can also be associated with ambiguity, error and foolishness by people who value rules, procedure and practicality more highly. So the locks to creativity are carried around in the heads of people which we can more generally call beliefs. We think that van Oech's title is very apt, and perhaps it might help to shift some of these beliefs that are serving to keep creativity locked up for fear of breaking a grown-up, stable and risk-free existence.

■ Action for innovation

Having broken down the blockages, unlocked ability, aligned purpose and positioned innovation at the core of identity, the final element is process – the mobilisation of teams using a project methodology that will support the drive for innovation.

There are many established approaches to choose from, ranging from simple 'quality action teams' to more sophisticated project management methodologies. The section on teams in Chapter

6 will no doubt provide some guidance here, and so we will offer a number of principles to suggest how to mobilise teams for innovation.

Principles for action

The first principle is involvement – rather than import an off-the-shelf solution, create your own. This will bring people together and reinforce the value your organisation is placing on involvement, creativity, innovation and teamworking.

The second principle is talk about it everyday, otherwise it will remain at the back of people's minds and they will not think to engage in creative processes.

During my time at Computacenter I was involved in designing the training for an approach to managing projects which had been created for their specific environment. It was the result of a creative process involving many people, and drawing on their collective experience of managing complexity and ambiguity in the world of desktop computing. Other companies were using a well-established methodology called PRINCE meaning 'Projects in a Controlled Environment'. The person leading this new initiative in Computacenter was one of the more insightful project managers at that time, and he came up with the acronym PRIDE meaning 'Projects in a Dynamic Environment'. The end product of their labour suited their needs completely. Initially designed to manage client projects, it was so successful that it soon came to be used for all manner of in-house projects. I even used it to manage some training projects, such was its flexibility. The people involved with this were, I believe, breaking the rules and creating new paradigms for project management. They were risk takers, stimulated by challenge, and looking to create something different which was more useful and effective than anything else which existed. The competition settled for much less than this.

Out of the many ways to mobilise teams, there is one more prin-ciple to observe: all procedures should increase choice. If the structure designed to deliver innovation is too prescriptive people will not feel that they can contribute freely, and so choice will be reduced. The challenge here is to build a well-recognised method-ology that frees people from the overhead of bureaucracy, yet pro-vides them with the tools and channels necessary to deliver innovation to the business. Make it OK to be wacky and use an assortment of creative tools. Allow people to loosen up and enjoy being creative. Fresh ideas rarely come from sensible minds, it is often an irrational thought from a relaxed and playful mind that sparks the first creative idea which leads to the next creative idea, and the next, until finally up springs a workable idea, one that can be innovated successfully.

■ Innovation alignment questionnaire

1　How does your organisation's purpose encourage innovation?

_____

_____

2　How does it inhibit innovation?

_____

_____

3　Is the organisational identity one that supports innovation, and if so, how?

_____

_____

4　How do the corporate values support innovation?

_____

_____

5　How do they discourage it?

_____

_____

6   What other elements of the climate in your organisation are impor-
      tant to encouraging innovation?

   _____

   _____

7   What elements are inhibiting it?

   _____

   _____

Note

1 Roger van Oech (1983) *A Whack on the Side of the Head*. Thorsons.

10

CHANGE

Introduction

One of the most powerful applications of the universal alignment model is helping people in organisations to create and navigate change. It is probably the most written about topic on the management bookshelf, yet few organisations seem to have found a solution to the paradox we call change; there are those that cannot seem to get enough of it, and those that would rather have less. To put this peculiarity into perspective, a reflection on the past fifteen years of our endeavours searching for evermore effective methods of managing change has brought us to the conclusion that *different ways of thinking*, rather than *different ways of acting*, would be a more useful starting point. And so in continuing this quest, to find new ways of aligning individuals with higher purpose, and to create aligning processes that help us move to a more desirable place than the one we currently occupy, we are using a different lens with which to view the entire topic of change.

We began the book with a description of alignment and continued with an exploration of each of the alignment distinctions. By now we trust that our application of the universal model to the main foci of organisations is demonstrating not only its relevance, but also its simplicity and flexibility of use. So while application of the alignment model facilitates purposeful change, we have intentionally avoided the word 'change' as a central theme. With that said, we will now tackle the paradoxical topic of the millennium by exploring some important themes.

The process of change

Let us begin by trying to understand the thinking we have created for ourselves through listening to the experts over the years. The model much used in business schools describes two forces of change: driving forces and restraining forces. This Newtonian principle teaches us that for every action there will be an opposed reaction of equal force. Applied to an organisational context, for every person that pushes for change, there will be someone who will resist it with equal force. This axiom has not deterred us from attempts to bring about change, but it may help to understand why such poor progress has been made, and why so many theories have emerged.

The academic thrust of 'change management' begins with the perceptions formed from Newtonian principles, that resistance to change exists. The organisational development school is based mainly on the principles that there are ways of reducing resistance to change before implementation, first of all 'unfreezing' the current state, making the desired change and then 'refreezing' to establish new norms of operating. Steady state changes to steady state. This approach to managing change is based on a particular perception of the world. It assumes the purpose of change is to move from here to there, from a 'not good' place to a 'better' one. Change is a step with the purpose of making a discrete, definable, one-off improvement.

In this chapter we suggest an alternative perception, one that allows us to consider other approaches unbound by how we currently think about change. We encourage you to think from a different perspective, since the principles of action and reaction, or of driving forces versus restraining forces, serve to reinforce the paradox which is itself limiting. In contrast to more established theories, our approach is not to break the paradox, but to accept, respect and understand it before joining others' perceptions in a learning process. First, we take a detour to the world of athletics, courtesy of the Michael Johnson website:

> The great ones make it look easy. When American Michael Johnson blazed across the finish line to win the Olympic gold in the 400 metres, he was 10 metres in front of the pack and accelerating. No runner has ever dominated this most demanding of all races so completely or made it look so simple. A few critics even suggested that he was holding back, conserving energy for

the 200 metres three nights later. Point taken. Johnson's winning time in the 200 shattered the world record – obliterated it for the ages.

Imagine Michael Johnson running in a 200-metres race, powering around a bend in the track. In freeze-frame his body appears at about 30 degrees from the upright with his head cocked still further in to one side. His point of contact with the ground is his outside leg and his arms are held in what seem to be two separate and unnatural positions, one stretched out front, the other trailing behind. This is a picture of great imbalance, if we look in the moment, but we are looking at a snapshot of a process not a still picture of a moment. And so, we can appreciate the athletic grace of the image. Is Johnson out of balance, misaligned? The moment captures his posture in such a way as to suggest that if he were not moving he would certainly fall over. Yet the success of this outstanding athlete, a multiple world and Olympic gold medalist in both the 200 and 400 metres, is due, in part, to his exquisite balance and running style. His balance is not static but dynamic, in every moment he is moving forward and reorienting his posture for the next stride. There is no steady state, rather, there is continual motion. And in this motion his mind and body are fully involved and committed to the task of succeeding, a task for which he must continually put himself out of alignment, leading himself forward and sidewards. So Johnson is perfectly balanced and aligned – aligned in motion.

And we are reminded of how this is also true for organisations, that:

Change is a continual process of alignment to a common purpose.

It is not a step-change from this state to a new state, requiring management intervention of unfreezing and refreezing. This is precisely what we need to be moving away from. Our purpose in our organisations, regardless of industry or activity or sector, might be more aptly phrased as Michael Johnson would phrase his own, 'to be moving faster than anyone else'.

The concept of change

If we accept that we must continually be thinking about change, then *how* we think about it is going to be vital. It becomes interesting to explore how we might reframe our entire understanding of change. How would we apply a new framework of thinking to organisations? What new language would replace the current language keeping our paradigm of change fixed in our minds?

What we are considering is quite simple in statement, yet profound in meaning. It is like the joke where a traveller asks a local the way to Kilkenny only to hear the reply, 'If I wanted to get to Kilkenny I wouldn't be starting from here.' In this chapter we are inviting you to review the thinking and language you employ when dealing with change; finding a different place to begin from so that you have a freer orientation of thinking. We know that once this is achieved the concepts and language of alignment become a flexible, dependable and highly effective toolkit.

There is no shortage of new theories for those who are curious enough to join the quest for a new paradigm. We can draw upon quantum physics and chaos theory to expand our awareness, and equally we can take lessons from ancient philosophers, people who were clearly ahead of their time, whose theories are receiving increasing scientific approval. It is interesting to notice how the leading theories of physics developed by such eminent thinkers as Einstein, Bohm, Bohr and Pribram[1] to name but a few, are tuning in to similar concepts of reality described by shamans some 5000 years ago. Both camps seem to be approaching the conclusions that everything is connected to everything else.

It is not possible to change one part of a system without affecting other parts.

Thinkers in the field of organisational development and management are now accommodating these possibilities in the search to identify the fundamental principles upon which business is organised. Let us follow one particular instance of this. The following quotation is taken from the *Tao te Ching*[2] written around the first century AD offering much advice to the rulers of the day in China. This particular extract draws parallels with the leadership challenges we face in business today:

> In the pursuit of learning one knows more every day; in the pursuit of the way one does less every day. One does less and less until one does nothing at all, and when one does nothing at all there is nothing that is undone. It is always through not meddling that the empire is won. Should you meddle, then you are not equal to the task of winning the empire. (Book 2, p. 108)

One of the constraints to progress is the meddling manager, afraid to delegate, untrusting of other people's abilities to do a good job, and keeping tight control over the way tasks get done. Meddlers might take this point of principle from Lao Tzu: how can we not meddle, how can we do less and less, what is involved in doing nothing? Modern management thinking says the sign of an effective manager is one who empowers others, and in so doing creates her own redundancy. We can learn much from the texts left to us by the great philosophers since very little is new in the realm of human relationships, commitment and motivation. We may have advanced our understanding of the world through the sciences, but the essence of human emotions has changed hardly at all. The simplest of essential lessons stand the test of time. Before continuing our journey to discover a different way of thinking, let us explore some of the factors which keep us rooted in the existing mindset.

We can learn much from the texts left to us by the great philosophers since very little is new in the realm of human relationships, commitment and motivation.

Simple is not the same as easy

As a society we are surrounded with complexity. Complexity is a necessary part of modern life, it is tied into each step forwards for us, the human race. This much is clear. Yet when we begin to associate complexity with progress we are making a dangerous link, because we may perhaps lose the facility to challenge it as rigorously as we did in the past. We have begun to accept that the most meaningful and effective learning has to be bound in numerous pages of detailed and complex information. Yet great leaps can be achieved when we take seriously the profundity of the simplest of things.

Let us think about a hoary old chestnut for all of us business people, time management. When we run our personal effectiveness seminars, time management is almost always identified as one of the most important improvements people want to make. And people are conditioned to look for complex solutions. Binders with multiple dividers, cross-referencing different sections of information, or computer packages that allocate and count time, prioritise and remind us what activity we should be occupied with at different stages of the day. Yet when we question people in more detail they quickly identify that organising complex numbers of variables is not the major stumbling block for them. Much more often the big gains in effectiveness come from two learnings, both remarkably simple.

> Yet great leaps can be achieved when we take seriously the profundity of the simplest of things.

We are indebted to Stephen Covey for bringing to the attention of the business world the distinction between importance and urgency. By understanding this simple distinction and using it to review all of the tasks which could occupy our time, we can see our priorities so much more clearly. Covey expands upon this idea in *First Things First*,[3] a book well worth reading.

The second learning is about the quality of our attention. We are so bombarded with information and demands for our attention throughout any one day that we need to discriminate what we pay attention to and how we do so. The ability to focus on a single issue, fully and completely, without diversion or interruption is seldom practised, at least according to our seminar participants. This quality of attention, that is, focused concentration, is actually a very simple way of improving time management. So many tasks can be completely dealt with in very short periods of time given this practice. Rather than further complexity, two simple lessons can make a huge difference.

That is not to say that the incorporation of that learning will be simple. Often, the simplest lessons are the last to be learned, because they take so much more energy and commitment to integrate into our behaviour, and it seems easier to continue the current pattern of behaviour which is, of course, habitual. Accumulation of facts and information is a much easier process than the assimilation of new behaviour into our repertoire of skills. Changing habits requires conscious thinking, consistent activity and discipline. I have recently been helping a friend who wants to improve her posture which she holds with a slight hunched back and often with tightly folded arms. She said that her previous posture was 'comfortable'. I suggested she think of it as habitual, and said, ' When you do these exercises and adopt a more healthy posture that will soon become habitual, and you may find that also comfortable. And it will certainly be more healthy for you.'

> Often, the simplest lessons are the last to be learned, because they take so much more energy and commitment to integrate into our behaviour, and it seems easier to continue the current pattern of behaviour which is, of course, habitual.

> Changing habits requires conscious thinking, consistent activity and discipline.

Wherever we have witnessed giant leaps in learning with tangible results flowing from the learning, it has been where the person has concentrated on a simple principle and worked at developing and mastering a skill in simple stages. The most impoverished learning we have found is where a person concentrates on acquiring increasingly complex knowledge and fails to internalise simple principles. This results in the familiar situation where a person knows all there is to know about a subject, how to manage well or to delegate effectively perhaps, but does not actually engage in the activity themselves.

Coaching is a good example. Good coaching is based on the simple principle that the best way to help someone improve performance is to encourage his own exploration of ideas and solutions, rather than give him the answers. The relatively simple skills involved are listening, understanding and questioning. Those managers that succeed in becoming great coaches are the ones that believe in the principle to the extent that they work at developing the skill each day. A high level of skill requires the complete integration of both principles and techniques. Less successful learners often fail to take on board the meaning of the principles involved in new methods.

'Simple' often gets confused with 'easy', yet the simplest changes can be the most difficult because it is all too easy not to change. One of the exercises we use to demonstrate this in our workshops is to ask people to move their wristwatch to the opposite wrist. This is so uncomfortable for some people that they become desperate to return it to the original wrist within minutes. Even such a small change as this can be very uncomfortable for some people.

Fragmentation and wholeness

Our experience in helping others to become more effective learners reveals many human frailties, perhaps they are ways of coping with the changing environment. As the world increases in its complexity we tend to cope by compartmentalising the external environment into manageable units. In our organisations we create structures and divisions, operating units, functional boundaries and work processes with inputs and outputs. This fragmentation process allows us to focus on one limited area of activity at any one time so that we can understand it and improve it. One of the problems with fragmentation is the 'horse with blinkers' effect, that while we may be focused on a particular view of the organisation we may not be considering the wider picture.

The science of organisational development has advanced to offer many alternatives for improving performance. TQM, reengineering, and other similar approaches have been implemented, and many such initiatives bear results, but we find it is done most often in a fragmented way. Improving one part of an organisation without considering the wider system it belongs to is to take a fragmented approach. Systems thinking has helped to enrich our understanding of the wider consequences of tinkering with parts of a whole, reminding us of the way in which all of the different elements of a system are interlinked. Peter Senge[4] gives us a brilliant insight into the ways in which systems thinking impacts on organisations in *The Fifth Discipline*. Two of the principles he proposes seem to demonstrate very vividly the dangers of fragmented thinking.

Systems thinking says that:

Cause and effect are not closely related in time and space.

This is true in all sorts of surprising ways. How often do we connect the escalating safety problems of an overcrowded airspace with booking our package holiday? Is anyone doing anything about this?

Negative attitudes of employees are sometimes responses to memories of past management methods, and the current management, more open than the old regime, becomes frustrated at the continuing resistance to ideas for improvement. In one organisation we have worked with, any change proposal from management was met with a reminder of the 30 people who were made redundant in 1976.

The upshot of this is that we need to widen our gaze, to look beyond the bounds of the obvious into the darker or more remote corners of the system. Doing this will ensure we have factored in all of the influences over the situation that we wish to change.

Small changes can produce big results.

But the areas of highest leverage are often the least obvious. I guess this has been in popular knowledge for many years, at least since someone penned the popular ditty about the want of a nail losing the shoe, and the consequent lost war. The alignment model gives us some really good clues about where the highest leverage might be found. Changes at the higher level distinctions affect those beneath, that is how the model works. An example that demonstrates this well came to me in the comments of a training manager from Iceland, the UK frozen food retailer. What had impressed him was not the rhetoric that surrounded some planned changes, or the glossy communication that heralded the new dawn. For him it was to see one of the directors of the business, well-known for his obstinacy and intolerance of other people's ideas, demonstrating an entirely new behaviour – listening and involving others at meetings. It was no longer a question of whether or not the changes would happen, they had arrived. The leverage in this organisation existed in helping some senior people with high visibility to act in accordance with the professed values. We respectfully submit that this is one method guaranteed to work in almost every organisation!

Patterns of interaction

Walking my dog one day, I reflected on how her routine stick fetching could be abruptly interrupted by something more important such as the sight of a rabbit. And how true this is for humans. A regular 14-hour day, 6-day week, can become habitual until something more important takes hold of our thinking, such as the increasing needs of a young and growing family, or the death of a loved one. There are specific patterns, rehearsed ways of dealing with situations which we fall back on time and time again in our responses to an ever changing world. We need to be able to recognise these patterns in ourselves and in others if we are to rise above their hold on us, otherwise we might compare our attempts to engineer change with the futility of throwing the stick for my dog and shouting 'sit'. If I want my dog to sit I must not throw a stick at the same time.

If we want people to think for themselves we must refrain from giving them solutions.

Some of the patterns, when discussed, will be readily recognised. They are so much a part of human behaviour that we tend to overlook their importance in any change initiative, yet the simplicity they offer our understanding is considerable.

■ The sameness / difference continuum

Some people like their lives to have a high level of routine with a smattering of difference. Holidays are taken at the same location, the same route is taken to work each day, and it is comforting to know that everything at work will be the same as it was yesterday. A job will last many years before feeling the need for a change, perhaps 20 years or more for someone who has an extreme need for similarity in their life. Change is OK as long as it contains many features similar to those in the present state of affairs and if it is introduced very gradually. People with a strong need for similarity in their lives will be motivated towards situations where the need for sameness will be satisfied. Too much change can create stress.

At the opposite end of this continuum are people who value difference. They go to a different place each year for their holiday, use a variety of routes to work and look for alternative, non-routine ways of doing things. Change is actively sought, sameness avoided. Job changes can be as frequent as yearly and dramatic fast change is positively embraced. A high need for difference in life motivates a person to seek situations where this need will be satisfied. People who relish difference can be perceived as confusing and problematic by those preferring a stable existence full of sameness. The opposite is also true.

You may be plotting your own preferences along this continuum, or those of the people in your social and work life. Figure 10.1 shows the range of possibilities along the continuum. These preferences can be noticed in the approach people take to their jobs, and to overlook or dismiss them is to discount one of the chief causes of paradox in organisations. Research conducted by Rodger Bailey[5] indicates the following distribution in the work context: sameness 5 percent; sameness with some difference 65 percent; difference 20 percent; difference with some sameness 10 percent.

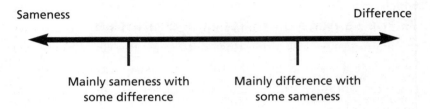

Figure 10.1
The sameness/
difference
continuum

■ The options / procedures continuum

If you were to compare our company brochure with a selection from other companies operating in the same market, one of the things you will notice is a lack of written detail. The ways in which we work with clients are varied, and through our high value for innovation we are constantly finding new ways of helping people to achieve their goals. This may cause us to appear somewhat vague in our brochure about the specifics of what we do – we like to keep our options open for the benefit of our clients. This gives us more choice in designing solutions to suit their culture. In contrast to this some companies produce brochures with lists of what they do itemised to the letter. This is the approach of a more procedurally oriented organisation.

People who prefer to keep options open like to have a choice, and might only take the choice when all options have been explored. A typical options pattern for a meal out is to visit a selection of restaurants in an area of town until either all the restaurants have been visited, or hunger forces a choice. At its worst, in an organisation this pattern can lead to unfinished projects and procrastination.

In contrast, a procedural pattern seeks a sequence of logical steps with which to complete a task. Life can be ordered by listing what needs to be done for any situation, by a numbered or bulleted list. In the absence of a written procedure life becomes stressful, ambiguous and difficult. Again, think what happens when people from opposing ends of the continuum work jointly on a project. They tend to misunderstand one another and may disrespect the other's style of working. This is a very simple fact which explains many personality clashes at work, and is yet another contributor to organisational paradox. Figure 10.2 shows the main preferences along this continuum. Research conducted by Rodger Bailey indicates the following distribution in the work context: options 40 percent; procedures 40 percent; equal options and procedures 20 percent.

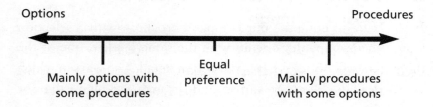

Figure 10.2
The options/
procedures
continuum

There are of course many other motivation patterns and our intention here is not to detour into the area of human psychology, rather to pull these two specific and highly influential patterns of behaviour into the frame, because of their particular relevance to change in organisations. Knowing how these patterns create a push–pull effect to change, it is no wonder that change continues to be a hot topic in business schools and enterprises. An organisation with too many people creating options may lack the structure and procedures necessary to be effective operationally, and vice versa – a highly procedural organisation may have effective internal operations, but lack the creativity to sustain a competitive edge. A similar result can be assumed from imbalances of sameness/difference motivation patterns.

Alignment for change

Our love of complexity, the tendency to look at fragments not wholes, and these two particular behavioural patterns are all examples of how we are somewhat rooted in our thinking about change. Earlier in the chapter we suggested that change be better embraced as a welcome and continuing factor of organisational life, even of life itself. What we are keen to explore now is how that approach to change would appear if plotted against the universal alignment model.

> Our purpose now as an organisation is to move faster, to change more rapidly and to stay ahead of whatever constitutes competition.

■ Purpose of change

Consider the purpose that we glimpsed earlier when we considered the analogy of Michael Johnson, the purpose of moving faster than anyone else, and how this fundamentally rejigs our whole thinking. Our purpose now as an organisation is to move faster, to change more rapidly and to stay ahead of whatever constitutes competition. If we think of the competition in the market place, we need to make ourselves more attractive to our customers than anyone else. We can do this by adapting or shaping; in short by doing whatever is required for us to continue to be the supplier of choice. We will explore partnership, look at building dependence into the relationship or set up some reciprocity to make the bond between us more secure. Whatever it takes. We need to be continually alert, and continually adapting, in order to retain our position.

> In the public sector, or other organisations where the competition is less obvious, we need to fight to beat the forces of inertia and decline that affect any system that is not changing and revitalising itself.

In the public sector, or other organisations where the competition is less obvious, we need to beat the forces of inertia and decline that affect any system that is not changing and revitalising itself. Without change the current way of operating will, in today's rate of development, become antiquated and slow in a matter of a few years, if that. Changing here means adapting to the latest technologies, systems and methods in order to be most effective, perhaps to spend public finance most prudently, or to maximise the use of a fixed budget.

Whatever our circumstances, we need to become professional at changing, at moving. If our purpose is to keep moving forwards in our own field, then our thinking will continually remain ahead of what we are doing today, leading us on to our next steps.

This paradigm is subtle, perhaps too much so. We look at the Japanese approach of kaizen, continuous improvement, classifying it as a process improvement technique. Yet it is also a philosophy, so fundamental that we can easily overlook its importance. Continuous improvement is continuous change, it is quiet dissatisfaction with the present, the underlying knowledge that we can have better, improved, more effective ways of doing what we do. Continuous improvement, embedded as a purpose at every level of the organisation, will produce the champions, the Michael Johnsons of business.

> Continuous improvement, embedded as a purpose at every level of the organisation, will produce the champions, the Michael Johnsons of business.

■ Identity for change

How does a person who creates change think about himself? This is an important issue for any organisation which clearly decides to put a high value on continuous change. What does this mean for people whose job, up to that time, was to keep things in place? And how many people in the organisation are performing a role such as this? How will these people be included in the change?

One common answer to this situation is to implement a ready-made programme of improvement, perhaps TQM or an equivalent. To this approach can be bolted all kinds of incentives, awards and merits for improvements to processes. Yet people who naturally create change need none of these external devices, they have a strong sense of identity as someone who does things differently, a pioneer breaking new ground, a shaper of the environment perhaps. Not everyone will want to be a pioneer, that is for sure, but by creating a strong identity for the organisation through metaphor, symbol and language, people will find their own natural level at which to create change. For some, it may be small incremental improvements to processes, for others whole new ways of looking at products or markets. The main thing is that individuals can connect with the organisational identity, and feel a part of it.

There are some consequences of ignoring identity. Apart from the obvious external effects of a weak identity influencing customer and market perception, the internal effects on employees are often overlooked. A weak identity makes it more difficult for people to define and connect with a purpose, and this creates a reduced sense of belonging leading to low commitment. Even worse when change is on the agenda is the feeling of moving between two unclear identities. Time spent with a team shaping, describing and trying on a new identity will be time well-invested. This is where the strongest bonds between employees are made, and where high performing teams draw their energy.

> For change to produce desired results the people involved must feel that the proposed change will have value for them.

■ Values for change

For change to produce desired results the people involved must feel that the proposed change will have value for them. Without this you get low commitment to making it work. At the most fundamental level we suggest that our approach, substituting conventional change with alignment, has four key values: involvement, respect, adventure and curiosity, all of which can be deeply imbedded into the culture. The degree to which these values are integrated will affect an organisation's ability to keep aligned with its purpose, however frequently it may change. In attempting to integrate these values there may be blocks to overcome, the most obstructive being power and control which we discuss after taking a look at the four key values.

Involvement

Involving people makes them crusaders for the cause, rather than conscripted troops on a forced march. All of our experience, and we suspect yours too, points to this. We know this, yet the most interesting question that remains is: how do we involve people?

> There is growing concern in our local community that education in state schools is far from effective. We know that learning technology has advanced to a stage far beyond what most schools recognise, and we want to bring about change. We have looked at the conventional methods of change via teachers, governors and politicians, but their perception of what is 'good' in education is far from that of the parents. Various attempts to launch an agenda for improvements have been unsuccessful, and we are almost resigned to abandon the impetus to introduce leading edge methods of learning into state education. What we have noticed is how structured and controlled the process of parental involvement is. With such a rigid approach it is difficult to get ideas off the ground. The system is geared to protecting the current school administration, rules and regulations, any changes being very small indeed, mainly restricted to peripheral issues only. Have you ever felt this way about something? Motivated to change things, but without a way of getting involved? The result is often frustration, or reduced interest in the subject. Motivation certainly plummets.

Attempts to involve people in organisations are varied, ranging from the highly structured and formal to the loose and informal. The patterns of interaction mentioned earlier reveal the different preferences people have for working methods. The more structured approaches tend to find favour with people who are more inclined to value a procedural, well-structured system, whereas unstructured approaches are favoured by people who prefer difference and options.

> **Our commitment to a cause is strongest when we have been involved at the highest level of relationship.**

The different ways in which people can be involved in organisations can be described with the help of Figure 10.3. Is it true that
the most adaptive organisations are necessarily those with the
highest level of involvement? And the balance between involvement and disordered chaos is one that we must strike, there is no
simple right and wrong here. When we reflect upon our own
experience of involvement we know that our commitment to a
cause is strongest when we have been involved at the highest level
of relationship, of deciding the nature of our own involvement
and interaction within the group. So how is it that we often miss
this important fact when involving others in our organisations?
People commit to ideas and plans more readily, and with stronger
emotional engagement, when they have been involved at the level
of idea generation or higher. The lower the level of involvement,
the lower the commitment, energy and drive. Why not involve
people in designing their own system of involvement? That way
the organisation gets something that is middle ground and suits
the majority. It is also more likely to produce results, having been
created by the people and not foisted onto them from the lofty
heights of the management fad seminar.

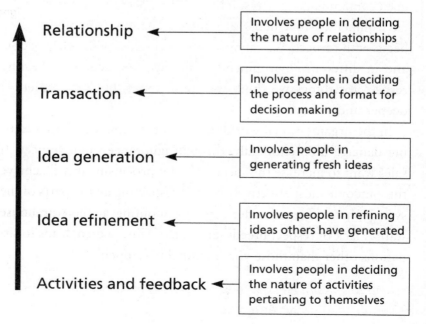

Figure 10.3
Levels of
involvement

So it would make sense, in the context of a continuous alignment process, to involve people at the highest level possible, harnessing their energy and commitment for the well-being of the organisation.

High involvement → internal commitment + high level of self-motivation
Low involvement → external commitment + low level of self-motivation

Involvement seems to go hand in hand with another key value, respect.

Respect

Respect is something we often learn through experience, after we have done some damage through disrespect. Wherever you look in the global environment you will find this is true. On many continents, indigenous tribes have suffered greatly as a result of an invader's disrespect for their culture and environment. Native American Indians, Aboriginals and Africans are glaring examples of this. Many natural habitats for endangered species are being destroyed as a result of disrespect. The air we breathe has been contaminated as a result of our disrespect for our own environment. Movements to improve all these situations begin with respect. We cannot hope to co-exist with other people and in different environments unless we first acquire a healthy respect for things we think we know about, but which merit a deeper understanding.

In the organisational world we act in the same way, often causing damage unintentionally, through ignorance or disrespect. If sales want to increase the speed of order processing it will achieve this outcome most effectively by first respecting all the parts of the system that influence orders, not by shouting at the warehouse staff. A lack of respect breeds ignorance. This, in turn, leads to situations other than those you intended to happen.

The only journey is the journey within.
[Rainer Maria Rilke]

A lack of respect breeds ignorance.

Unless we respect other people for their own unique experience of the world and for the original contribution they can bring then involvement is a sham. When we respect them, and want them to have an opportunity to contribute and enjoy the processes they are involved in, then new possibilities emerge. But, to quote one of our clients, 'This respect stuff ain't so easy to do.' It requires us to suspend a good deal of our own thinking. Because of its fundamental importance in all of our dealings with other people we return to the subject with some practical ideas in Chapter 11.

Adventure

The more we advance as a race, the more we become averse to taking risks. The phenomenal size of the insurance market is testament to this fact. If you have enough money you can insure just about anything against damage, loss or theft. Products come with extended guarantees and no-quibble refunds. Retailers know that reducing risk is one way of getting us to part with our hard-earned cash. We do not like surprises that could be costly, and we like to stay comfortable, secure with our loved ones, and our material possessions. Yet all this suggests a need for safety and familiarity, both of which go against the grain of change. Having an identity as a pioneer or a shaper of the future without a value for adventure is highly unlikely to produce much in the way of innovation.

Work can be invested with importance, it can be deadly dull and very serious in some places. When we think of it in this way it encourages us to perfect the ways in which we operate, they have such importance to us. But what about the alternative? What if we see it, and talk about it as a game? Who wants to play? You bet people want to play; whether they can admit so in front of other people or not, we believe that people can readily play in all sorts of ways. We encourage people to throw off the sensible shackles of adulthood and get serious about playing. An adventure is just an extension of this philosophy. The adventure will take us to some great places, it will probably get us into one or two hairy scrapes, too, but what the heck? And who worries about preserving the form or the status quo when in the middle of a great big adventure? Being adventurous is to travel to new and unfamiliar territory, to do different things, to explore the unknown – to be curious to see what there is to see of the world – always asking questions, having an inquiring mind, free spirited and unfettered by rules and regulations. Work should be fun; suffering is an optional extra, but definitely one you provide for yourself.

> **Work should be fun; suffering is an optional extra, but definitely one you provide for yourself.**

Curiosity

I made a silent wish for my kids when each was born. It was simply this: that they grow up with a continuing sense of curiosity, a real thirst to know and to try different things, because I know that curiosity has taken me to some great places, led me through a number of different and valuable career steps and into some amazing new worlds of very different ideas. May it never die, and if it dims let me somehow be reminded of its value.

> **Fixed aspects melt into insignificance beside the excitement of the unknown or the unproven.**

If we are curious in our organisations then we will not be precious about where we are today, rather we will focus on where we might be in the future. Fixed aspects melt into insignificance beside the excitement of the unknown or the unproven. As a challenge, try just a couple of days in a state of intense curiosity, almost as a young child would. Ask the question 'why?' of as many things as you can, ask it of the answers you are given, and ask it to those answers, too. A few sacred cows of thought will be slaughtered all right.

Curiosity is another aspect of organisational life in such short supply that it demands much more coverage than we can afford in this work. We cover it in more detail as one of the principles of alignment in Chapter 11.

We now address the two values which are major obstacles to alignment.

Power

Organisational life is a natural habitat for the power lovers of the human species. Hierarchies, responsibility over others, status and position all pander to the weakness in us that thirsts for power.

Power serves the ego first.

And once obtained it is not easily given up, rather like Bilbo's ring it begins to affect the wearer, who can only reluctantly be parted from it. Is power a great driver for change? Well, at one level the answer might appear to be yes, after all one of the great ways to exercise power is illustrated by the 'I'm gonna make a few changes around here' school of succession.

It does not take long to realise, however, that this type of change is likely to contain some restrictions of fixed points that

Beware of power, and its close relation, control!

definitely will not be changing. And it is unlikely to have been truly consultative and almost certainly will not have involved people widely throughout the organisation. Power serves the ego first. This is its thirst and drive, over and above anything else. Organisations provide a rich source of nutrition for power-hungry people who may not go along too easily with attempts to introduce a more egalitarian way of life. Yet a need for power is a natural trait and should be respected. By respecting and understanding a person's need for power it will be much easier to work with her, and discuss the consequences of her actions. How do the actions resulting from the value 'power' help or hinder the efforts of the team? Beware of power, and its close relation, control!

Control

Organisations and people gripped by a need for control will never change and adapt as well or as rapidly as others unaffected by that value.

In our work with a major US manufacturer we see the rigid control structures and the very low level to which authority is devolved in the workforce. The manufacturer has an extremely successful business in its current format. Yet we fear for it when some far-reaching market changes arrive, as surely they will, because it is not training its people to be adaptable or flexible.

Companies have been increasingly turning to technology for ways of controlling their business, the proliferation of call centres and electronic messaging systems being examples of this. This is not such a bad thing, unless the technology also puts controls on the employees using it. In many situations this is, sadly, the case. We recently read about a large call centre, belonging to a household name insurance company, where operators were allowed only 20 seconds' break between telephone calls. They were monitored closely by supervisory staff, and offenders were given warnings. Needless to say, stress was high and so, too, was absenteeism.

The four values for change work to help the process of alignment. Respect helps people to understand how different parts of the organisation are aligned; involvement includes everyone in fulfilling the purpose; adventure and curiosity keep the organisation moving forward, reinventing its purpose according to how it wants to shape the environment it is in. The degree to which any organisation is able to integrate these values will of course depend upon the amount of power and control exerted on employees. The smart organisations will do their utmost to reduce these obstacles.

■ Language of change

Language is the way we begin to transfer our internal thoughts. It is the way we try to allow others to glimpse our own map of the world, it is the medium by which our ideas can be shared by others. The words we choose are a reflection of our thoughts;

> Not only do our words reveal our thoughts but our words can also begin to shape our thoughts.

never a complete or a truly accurate reflection, but nonetheless an approximation of our own reality. Language has its limitations, it can seldom reveal the richness and texture of our thoughts, except perhaps through the pen of a poet or a writer, skilled in using words to trigger other people's thinking. Not only do our words reveal our thoughts but our words can also begin to shape our thoughts.

Observing the way people use language is a great insight into the way they think, and we intend to show that by using language purposefully you can guide your own thinking and also help others with their train of thought. We could write another book on this subject, but for our purposes here we intend to provide the reader with an orientation to the type of language you would hear in a company committed to alignment as an integral part of its culture.

These are essential questions which, if used frequently, will prevent misalignment from taking root and creating inertia. The key phrases you will hear most often can be categorised under three stages of any change process:

- deciding purpose, desire and outcomes
- learning from experience
- being different in pursuit of your purpose.

After providing some examples for each stage we will share some more common phrases which will help to free up anyone's thinking.

Purpose / desire / outcome language

The intention of these questions is to bring clarity to situations by revealing the fundamental purpose behind any working relationship. They also challenge the current situation and begin the process of introducing difference.

- What do I want to achieve?
- What do we want to achieve together?
- What is our purpose here?
- What do we want as a result of pursuing our purpose?
- What is the purpose of this activity?
- In what way does our purpose fit with the organisation's purpose?
- How do our combined purposes complement each other?
- Do the outcomes of our efforts help others to fulfil their purpose?

Learning from experience

One of the outcomes of working in a complex environment is a rich and varied experience. This also brings one of the main blocks to progress – time invested in reflecting on this experience and learning from it. In many organisations, this investment is clearly insufficient. The following questions will help to reveal the essential elements of experience with which to focus the learning effort.

- What activities contributed to our fulfilling our purpose?
- What activities added value (no value) to the organisation?
- What activities added value (no value) to us personally?
- What did we enjoy? What didn't we enjoy?
- What did we excel at? What didn't we excel at?
- What have others said about our performance?
- How are we different now? In what ways are we changing?
- In what ways are our skills developing?
- How would we describe our full range of capability?
- Have we been stretched?
- How have we worked as a team?
- In what ways have we been adventurous?
- Have we taken risks, or have we been playing safe?
- In what ways have we progressed through being curious and inquisitive?
- How many times have we questioned convention and orthodoxy?
- How many times did we challenge the rules?

Difference in the pursuit of purpose

Having drawn learning from experience the final stage consists of deciding to make changes. It will be useful to refer back to Chapter 2, and consider the various ways in which difference can be introduced. We suggest you avoid hamster wheel changes and doing more faster, and concentrate on the more intelligent ways of introducing change: game strategy (different action), mission impossible (different goals), and superheroes (different identity). The following questions cover these three options.

- What will we do differently the next time we approach that situation?
- What do our customers want us to do differently?
- What are we going to do more of?
- What are we going to do less of?
- What are we going to stop doing altogether?
- In what ways can we deploy our full capability to the purpose?
- Do we want to change our goals? What if we did – how might we change them?
- Are there other goals that fit more appropriately into the bigger picture?
- What else could we achieve for ourselves/the team/the company?
- Who are we now? In what ways are we evolving?
- How is our growing confidence and capability shaping who we are?
- What is the essence of what we are becoming? What metaphor describes us best?
- What parts of our identity are we going to leave behind us?

In your organisation, how often do you hear people using the kind of language which forms these questions? In our experience, most companies only ever consider questions like these when being facilitated by consultants, it does not form part of their everyday language. Perhaps this is one reason why consultants, particularly working in the area of change, are so much in demand – maybe they have all the best questions. When a company decides to challenge orthodoxy and perception, replacing conventional step-change with alignment, this is the type of language it will need to learn. It is a language which encourages movement at all of the alignment distinctions, and helps keep teams firmly anchored to a common purpose while giving them the maximum freedom to be creative. More conventional processes that plan for static futures act as periodic pattern interrupts evoking the response, 'Not another change!' By embedding the values of alignment – respect, involvement, and adventure into the culture – an organisation can move from the position of step-changes in response to 'flavour of the month' methods, to a longer lasting, smoother continuous improvement process.

More language for 'free thinking'

I recently decided to invest some time in rediscovering how to sing. As a kid I could sing, as a teenager and young adult my singing wasn't always appreciated by those within earshot. 'I can't sing in tune' was a phrase I often used, unless beaten to it by someone else telling me 'You can't sing.' I decided that I wanted to do something about this and so I began to use the magic word. Not the magic word, 'please', taught me by my parents, but the magic word, 'yet'. 'I can't sing tunefully, yet' is a world apart from 'I can't sing tunefully.' It moved me from being unable, stuck in my inability, to being in the process of learning, not yet a Domingo or a Sinatra, but no longer blocked. The sound of my voice didn't change overnight but my attitude sure did.

When facilitating creativity with groups we use a couple of linguistic devices to assist their thinking. Where we want to encourage participants to generate ideas, no matter how wacky or strange, it is really important that there is no sense of judgement or criticism for each others ideas. We disallow the words 'no' and 'but' and often use a specific exercise where a particular idea is passed around the group, developed and extended as each player picks up on what was said previously with the phrase 'yes … and'. The language here forces our thinking into seeing the merit of ideas and linking, stretching or improving them. Try the 'yes … and' response around the office for a couple of days, you will be amazed how it helps you to consider ideas in a new light.

The language of change is the language of movement and imperma-nence, of options and possibilities. 'We could do ...' opens the way for possi-bilities while 'We always do ...' is the language of permanence and necessity.

Start at the right place

> You must be the change you wish to see in the world.
> [Mahatma Gandhi]

We have mentioned some of the wrong places to start when think-ing about alignment, or change, and reflecting on the universal alignment model it should be clear that starting at the lower levels of action and capability rarely produces desired results. We should be thinking in terms of values and beliefs, or even better our sense of role and purpose. We may recognise the ways in which people differ, and consider these differences as a strength, even though we may have to adjust our communication style to accommodate them. Whatever principles we align against we must begin with a healthy respect and a curiosity to want to understand others' expe-riences. Having established this position it will be much easier to use the alignment model to facilitate thinking in a respectful way.

Here's a simple way of thinking about the effectiveness of changes in an organisation. Run through this for your company and see what you get.

First, list all the significant change initiatives that have occurred in your company over the past ten years (longer for a more established company):

_____

_____

_____

_____

_____

_____

_____

_____

_____

For each of these changes answer the following questions:

- To what extent has this change influenced the organisation's purpose?

  _____

  _____

- Has this initiative changed the identity of the organisation in any way?

  _____

  _____

- Have people adopted different values as a result of the change?

  _____

  _____

- Have there been any changes to the things people believe about their work?

  _____

  _____

- Has the change affected the organisation's capability in any way?

  _____

  _____

- What are people doing differently as a result of the change?

  _____

  _____

- In your opinion, was the change worthwhile, and has it added value for your customers?

  _____

  _____

Notes

1 Einstein, Bohm, Bohr and Pribram in Michael Talbot (1996), *The Holographic Universe*. HarperCollins.
2 Lao Tzu (1963) *Tao te Ching*. Penguin Classics.
3 Stephen Covey, A Roger Merrill and Rebecca R Merrill (1994) *First Things First*. Simon & Schuster.
4 Peter M. Senge (1990) *The Fifth Discipline*. Century.
5 Rodger Bailey (undated) *Words that Change Minds*. Kendall/Hunt.

PRINCIPLES FOR ALIGNMENT

- ■ Introduction
- ■ Eight principles for purposeful alignment
- ■ Learning to assimilate the principles

Eight principles for purposeful alignment

These principles have been tested, with our experience of both
future successful change in organisations and have been repeated
many times over the years by individuals, colleagues and definitions in similar periods.

1 Success starts with clarity of purpose
2 Alignment transforms energy into effectiveness
3 Respect is the beginning of understanding
4 Curiosity is the beginning of all difference.
5 Flexibility is the beginning of freedom

Introduction

We have articulated to some depth the way in which attitudes determine capability and regulate our action. It is now time to turn to the essence of making it work, and to this end we offer a set of core principles which will guide your activities as you begin to integrate alignment into the culture of your organisation.

> Principles are statements that serve as a lighthouse directs shipping through hazardous waters, showing the way ahead.

Whenever we are learning something new it is important to understand the key principles underlying the new idea or concept. Principles are statements that serve as a lighthouse directs shipping through hazardous waters, showing the way ahead. Principles act as fundamental laws concerning the nature of things, and they can tell us what to expect from certain actions, such as the principles explaining the theory of gravity, for example. In this way, principles crystallise our attitudes into a set of simple to understand and easy to follow laws. They are not a function of our individual thinking, like values and beliefs. Rather they are universal, true for all people and for all situations. The principles that follow govern the dynamics of purposeful alignment, and embrace a new framework for organisational change.

Eight principles for purposeful alignment

These principles have been formed from our experience of facilitating successful change in organisations, and have been endorsed many times over the years by numerous colleagues and clients involved in similar processes.

1 Success starts with clarity of purpose.
2 Alignment transforms energy into effectiveness.
3 Respect is the beginning of understanding.
4 Curiosity is the beginning of all difference.
5 Flexibility is the beginning of freedom.

6 Eduction is the key to releasing potential.

7 None of us is as smart as all of us.

8 Be thorough and unrelenting with issues.

■ Success starts with clarity of purpose

On a recent management development programme we met a senior manager from a large public service company in London. He was concerned that people occupying the seats of power in his organisation were holding back progress. Although a 'new face' for the service had been publicly announced, and investment had been put to infrastructure, training and publicity, these top operational managers didn't want to rock the boat with any changes because they were due to retire, very comfortably, in five years. There was a clear mismatch of purpose between those who were trying to shape the future for the organisation, and those in power who were shaping their own personal risk-free future in retirement. This situation led to confusion about the true purpose of the service, and was reflected in the reduced commitment of the workforce.

Articulating a higher purpose, perhaps connecting to a wider holistic view of the organisation, its markets and the industry is important. Equally important are the connections individuals make between this holistic purpose and their own sense of purpose at work. Facilitating this for others requires a solid foundation of inner purpose, clearly the missing component for the retiring managers in our example.

A strong sense of purpose will summon the drive for alignment, and although the purpose may be crystal clear in the mind of the originator, this is unlikely to be the case for others. Encouraging wider commitment to the purpose then becomes the challenge, because while it may be quite simple to describe your personalised sense of organisational purpose, and the value you attach to it, others will not have experienced the thought process you have been through to arrive there. So the task becomes one of facilitating this process for others and allowing them the opportunity to create something which may be somewhat different from your original idea.

Blocks to clarity of purpose

Thinking on the subject of purpose for a team, a company or a person might exist at one of several different stages.

In some instances purpose has never been specifically addressed by people. This is often the case in the small but important subgroups of an organisation. What is the purpose for our department, or for our function, this site, the factory or the shift? The reason for this is often simply the fact that it has never been identified as an important place to put attention.

Elsewhere we might find that some thinking about purpose has been done, once, some time ago. If this thinking is not being used, is not part of the daily language of the team, then it serves little or no valuable purpose, it is not valuable purpose. Purpose agreed, printed out and filed in the bottom drawer is time and energy wasted.

Sometimes purpose has been dictated by a central leadership. This can make it very difficult for that purpose to be recognised and adopted by the entire group affected.

Confusion and different interpretations are the traps awaiting any groups that do not carefully approach the activity of agreeing common purpose. Without malice or ill intention of any kind a group can end up with conflicting senses of its purpose, in a very short time. Unclear articulation, too much vagueness or lack of interpretation for the individuals concerned will all contribute to this possibility emerging.

People may commit to a purpose by what they say, while their actions can say something completely different. So when helping people to interpret purpose in their own terms, for their own roles, it pays to ensure they make appropriate connections with their behaviour.

How to create a clear purpose

In large organisations there will be a purpose for the organisation, and purposes for different functions. It is important that these link together and feed one another. The organisational purpose may be defined by an executive team, while each function will be responsible for agreeing its own. Equally important is the purpose of management, or co-ordinating teams, responsible for interfaces between functions. Let us consider a management team and look at six practical things the leader can do to achieve clarity of purpose.

1 Facilitate a common purpose – rather than the leader deciding the purpose, it is far more motivating for others when they have a part in creating a common purpose. Be a facilitator, avoid prescription.

2 Ask the team to paint a picture of what it will be doing to pursue the purpose.

3 Create a story together including ways in which the purpose will be pursued.

4 Draft a series of statements that accurately describe the purpose you have represented using picture and narrative.

5 Make sure that individuals are able to connect the purpose to personal needs and desires – the famous 'What's in it for me?' (WIIFM). Ask the team to seriously consider what the purpose will do for team members, both emotionally and developmentally. If connections are not easy to make, perhaps the purpose needs changing accordingly. Be open to the team's needs.

6 Finally, and most important, make reference to the purpose frequently and use it as a check for the degree to which any idea or action helps fulfil the purpose. Recite it at meetings to help clarify your role with people from outside your function.

■ Alignment transforms energy into effectiveness

A number of years ago I was sharing an office with a young sales manager called Mike. Mike would talk to me about the importance of investing in people, developing potential, and giving individuals direction and support to become successful at their job. This was also how Mike reflected on his own career development. The reality, I learned later, was quite different. His team members would tell me of how they felt tightly controlled, and afraid to make a wrong step for fear of embarrassment and reduced freedom. An example of how Mike would do this was displayed when he decided physically to move an underperforming salesperson to the desk adjacent to his so that he could keep an eye on what he was doing. Mike was a successful salesman, but he was new to management. His actions seemed somehow disconnected from his words of intent.

Alignment for individuals or for groups is the way to allow the maximum energy to flow into achieving the desired outcomes. And if we define effectiveness as the ratio between energy expended and outcomes reached, we can see that effectiveness also flows from alignment.

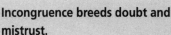

Incongruence breeds doubt and mistrust.

Lack of alignment or incongruence between what you say and what you do, or what you think and what you say, is communicated to others at an unconscious level through the tone of voice, body language, eye movements and gestures. People can often tell when someone has an internal misalignment, although they may not be able to say exactly what it is that is transmitting the incongruence signal. One thing is certain. Incongruence breeds doubt and mistrust. In organisations, misalignment means time and energy is spent doubting, conspiring, guessing or gossiping when that same energy could be deployed in moving the organisation forward.

Blocks to inner alignment

A number of blocks exist. Lack of alignment might exist because the person or the organisation is not yet consciously aware, or agreed, about the higher levels of thinking, particularly about purpose. Organisational politics, ambition and unmet personal desires also feature strongly here. Symptoms of this lack of alignment are varied and include:

• fear of failure
• low confidence in one's capability
• using the organisation as a game of chess in which tactical moves are deployed for personal advantage
• withholding information for personal career gain
• seeking personal credit for successes
• sweeping mistakes and problems under the corporate carpet
• setting others up for a fall
• playing defend/attack games with other functions.

These are all responses to the organisational environment, and seek to promote personal gain to the detriment of the organisation. Someone engaging in any of these tactics is unlikely to be congruent in her behaviour and may be distrusted. What often seems like a short-term strategy for self-promotion usually ends up with long-term misgivings – you reap what you sow.

Inner alignment requires the absorption of these eight principles, so that, in seeking to involve people and facilitate a collective alignment, there are no feelings of fear, vulnerability, mistrust, inadequacy or lack of control. Being completely aligned with these principles means that you are fully confident in the process of involvement, and hold the belief that people have the capability to evolve the organisation in appropriate and innovative ways. This sense of confidence will be recognised by others and interpreted without suspicion or distortion.

How to become internally aligned

Internal alignment for individuals is a quest. At the end of the quest lies a situation where purpose is known, and is being met in daily activity. In this place we would be content in our sense of ourselves, aware of our values and clear that they are being met. We would be realising larger parts of our capability and acting to bring our outcomes, our wants, into reality. This would be accompanied by a sense of balance, by acceptance, tolerance, and compassion for others.

This quest is a lifetime journey for many people. Such is the complexity of the world around us that even those who are deliberately seeking alignment take time to discover the answers that they need. In a parallel fashion the quest for alignment in organisations is a continuing one, a moving project. Remember that Michael Johnson is readjusting something like 200 different muscle groups on an ongoing basis to stay in balance and move forward simultaneously.

The 'how to' in both contests is about focusing deliberate attention on the distinctions of the alignment model. Begin to think in terms of purpose, identity and values. Begin to talk, to yourself and to others, in this language. Be deliberate in this. In organisations these are processes of meeting, of involvement, of consultation and of facilitated thinking.

For individuals this might involve any of the myriad approaches to personal development. The activities in this book and in our alignment workshops are designed to stimulate this process.

■ Respect is the beginning of understanding

A limiting belief we come across often when we are coaching clients is 'I don't respect people who disrespect me.' While we understand and respect how this stance may have been formed, it is nonetheless limiting because it puts the onus of respect with the other person. It is actually a belief, and is often held in place by some feeling of self-worth, creating a gulf of difference between the two disrespecting people. This is not a position of curiosity, flexibility, or any other resourceful state. It is a weak stance which serves only to deepen disrespect. When we have helped the client to change the belief it is amazing how quickly bridges in communication and understanding are built.

Respect is one of the most misappropriated of human qualities. We all think we know what respect is and how to show it, yet often our attempts are too shallow to make any difference to how someone feels. Respect is a basic human need. We all need to feel respected in some way, by other people. And respect is very similar to understanding, and the need to be understood. Respect and understanding are the foundations of meaningful relationships, whether between man and woman, parent and child or company and employee. Respect and understanding promote the self-worth which is needed to generate commitment to a worthy cause, and inner motivation to succeed. So respect is a starting point for any alignment activity, and there are some specific areas where respect needs to be directed.

> **Respect is a basic human need.**

> **Respect and understanding promote the self-worth which is needed to generate commitment to a worthy cause, and inner motivation to succeed.**

One of these areas is past experiences. The older people get, the more past experiences they have and the more their blood, sweat and tears have been invested in getting to their current position. In some companies, people have been mismanaged, mistreated, mistrusted and misled – creating a cynical and pessimistic view of management. These experiences must be understood and respected if you are to gain free, self-energised involvement. There is often so much past evidence of management incompetence and uncaring attitudes that addressing the imbalance requires patience and determination uncommon in many of today's organisations. A typical response to these imbedded attitudes is to blame the individuals, regardless of management's role in their making.

Another area where respect and understanding is often under-invested is in others' perceptions. We all usually have some notion about what needs to be done. Some people will feel more strongly than others about imperfections in structure, process, systems and methodology. Who decides whose ideas are best? Bringing these ideas out into the open and including them in healthy and rigorous debate is one way of showing respect. In theory, once lessons have been learned, it is more effective to leave the past behind and con-centrate effort on the present and the future. In practice, particu-larly where there is a history of non-involvement, time spent up-front understanding the past and respecting the issues people hold onto most protectively will later yield high returns in trust and commitment. Alignment activities require a healthy respect for what has gone before and for how people perceive their own needs and those of the organisation. Open and honest respect sets the foundations for designing the future together.

> Open and honest respect sets the foundations for designing the future together.

Blocks to respect

The most common block to respect has already been mentioned – limiting beliefs. To this we can add the following:

- Time – not taking enough time to show respect by listening.
- Priorities – urgent tasks prevent people from taking quality time to understand.
- Blaming – to blame is to excuse poor performance. To blame is also to direct negative emotions at the identity of a person or a group. Nothing useful ever comes from blaming, it is unre-sourceful to engage in blaming activities. It is far better to respect, understand, learn, decide and go forwards.
- Independence – we don't need them right now, so why waste time with them?
- Adversaries – sales vs engineering; production vs distribution; accounts vs everyone else.
- Experts – we know better than anyone else, and in many instances our thinking is 'I know best.'

How to be respectful

It can be difficult in the full flow of a busy day to break free of the urgent tasks that demand our attention, yet that is what we must endeavour to do. Showing respect is an act that takes time and begins with curiosity (Principle 4). If, instead of creating distance between people we do not understand through our brief encounters, we are curious to know about them and their environment we will at least begin in the right place. It must, therefore, be a priority for us. Making an effort to meet people where they are can be as easy as saying, 'Help me to understand your needs so that we can work together better', or 'I want to really understand your needs so that we can make progress here.' After asking the question we need to button our lip and listen – not shallow listening, but listening with an intense curiosity to know about the other person. Any personal judgement not grounded in fact, intervening in our thoughts, must be quashed. We can only truly respect a person when we have suspended our judgements about them.

■ Curiosity is the beginning of all difference

I recall coaching a young manager in the chemical industry, who complained that older people were always finding something to complain about. Their behaviour was difficult to manage, and the more they complained the more he became impatient with them. So I asked him to just listen, suspend his impatience and be curious to find out more about their past experiences – nothing more than this, for two weeks. On one occasion, a factory charge hand had objected to notices being displayed on the factory notice board announcing details of new people who had joined the company each month. These notices were a response from the factory workers complaining about all the new faces in the administration office – who were these people? When eventually the manager asked the charge hand why he objected to the notice, he replied, 'In my 25 years here no one has ever put my name up on a notice board.' Clearly, this behaviour was a response to a lack of recognition over the past 25 years revealed by the manager's newfound curiosity. Further attempts to understand the real reasons behind difficult behaviour eventually led to a deeper trust and respect between the manager and his people, and change became less of a stumbling block to progress.

Grudges are held from memories of past experiences, often bearing little relevance to the current situation. Many of them go unheard because it is all too easy to apportion blame on the attitude, rather than take the time to listen, understand and respect the ways in which people have been treated in the past. Curiosity is a basic prerequisite for so many aspects of working with other people. Learning requires a healthy curiosity to find out how to improve skills, and understanding is likewise dependent on a curious mind, as is respect. Any fact-finding task will require a generous amount of curiosity, and any creative thinking process would be flat without it.

Wherever people join together in common pursuit curiosity is an admirable quality.

Blocks to curiosity

In the middle of a busy working day it can be all too easy to work from our personal judgements and perceptions of how things appear to us. Often decisions are made from far too little evidence because time is allowed to rule the day. Sometimes curiosity can lead to mistakes, and in a culture disapproving of imperfection, curiosity may rarely find the opportunity to break through. Accepting what people say, taking things as true and accurate, never challenging the views of others, not taking the time to be thorough with important issues – these are all blocks to curiosity.

How to develop a healthy curiosity

- Be aware of when we are judging situations and people without supporting facts. Suspend personal judgements.
- Children are naturally curious. We tend to lose this natural curiosity as we become serious adults. Be childlike again in your search for discovering the unknown.
- Question information that paints an unclear picture. We can learn something from every single situation we are in.
- Ask more questions than you make statements.
- Ask people for more precise details if they generalise, or if they are vague when giving accounts of their experience.

■ Flexibility is the beginning of freedom

We have heard some people say that to be flexible is to be weak – giving in to others' opinions and wishes. People holding this view obviously hold a particular belief of how to be strong, and perhaps miss the point completely, which is more about having the freedom to choose than personal ego or belief. To be flexible is to be resourceful while inflexibility reduces choice and possibility. Flexibility is something which has to be continually worked at, learned, developed and integrated into everyday actions with other people. Flexibility gives us the freedom to choose our response in any situation. If we are slave to the hamster wheel, when things get tough freedom will elude us. To be free to choose other responses requires a flexibility of thinking and acting.

> Flexibility is something which has to be continually worked at, learned, developed and integrated into everyday actions with other people.

Blocks to flexibility

There are three main blocks to becoming more flexible:

1 Having a closed mind. The mind is like a parachute – it only works when open. Being the expert and knowing everything may do wonders for the ego, but it kills flexibility instantly.

2 Limiting beliefs. It is surprising how many places this crops up as a block to potential. Beliefs can be empowering but they can also provide a narrow tube with which to view the world. The latter gives rise to rigidity of thinking and behaviour.

3 Necessity. Too much need in one's life reduces the amount of possibility. Language containing statements of need, 'I/we/you need to …' implies that there is no choice. This reduces possibilities and therefore flexibility to do things differently.

How to become more flexible

There are five core skills to concentrate on for anyone wanting to develop flexibility of thought and action:

1 **Flexible thinking** – Learn to notice when you are limiting your flexibility through your thinking patterns. If you hold personal judgements about other people you are very likely to filter for information which reinforces your judgement. This is inflexible. Be open to challenge your own beliefs, and change them if they are constraining your ability to be flexible. Generate more options and look for possibilities wherever you find necessity. A willingness to change the way you think, including beliefs, values and perceptions will lead to increasing flexibility.

> Be open to challenge your own beliefs, and change them if they are constraining your ability to be flexible.

2 **Develop a range of responses to the environment** – Out of the four main responses we suggest that an ability to use the three most intelligent responses – game strategy, mission impossible and superheroes – will lead to further flexibility in the way problems and challenges are addressed. Becoming skilled at this requires practice, for individuals as well as teams. It is important to remember that superheroes can be active in the warehouse and factory as well as in the boardroom.

> It is important to remember that superheroes can be active in the warehouse and factory as well as in the boardroom.

3   **Adapt and shape** – Environments require reshaping from time to time in response to feedback from the environment. Every reshaping initiative must be accompanied by the adapting of processes to the changed environment. The two go hand in hand. We have mentioned how some people prefer to shape while others are more content to work on adapting. This means that, for any employee, regardless of status or position, there will be some situations where adaption to the initiatives of others is required, and other situations where reshaping is more appropriate. A flexible employee is one who respects the need for both responses.

> Every reshaping initiative must be accompanied by the adapting of processes to the changed environment.

4   **Facilitate a common view** – It takes flexibility to work in a group of people, where individuals are promoting their own ideas, to help formulate some new alternatives that have common appeal without imposing personal views of what you think should be happening. The skill required is that of a facilitator, a person who manages and directs the energy of others in a way that respects their needs, desires and outcomes. A resulting common view of a situation, problem, or solution is often different to your own, or any one person's. A skilled facilitator knows that an idea that has the commitment of the many is more likely to succeed than the idea with the commitment of the few. To facilitate a common view is a much more precious skill than that of persuading people to buy into a personal agenda.

> A skilled facilitator knows that an idea that has the commitment of the many is more likely to succeed than the idea with the commitment of the few.

5   **Patience** – This is one commodity that seems to be in short supply, and indeed in some organisations it has been extinct for some time. Long-term strategies often fall foul of short-term needs and impatience for results. This is very characteristic of action-oriented enterprises displaying the impetuosity of a child scrabbling for the last sweet in the jar. In some organisations, the value attached to immediacy can create the perception that patience is an undesirable quality – the word itself is outlawed from the managers' vocabulary. Yet patience is a virtue, and the best things come to those who wait. Those who satisfy themselves with immediate returns only will live a life full of short-term experiences which come to an end quickly – think of what this means for work, social life and family relationships.

The journey you will take to acquire these skills will cause you to question your own beliefs from time to time. Decide not to accept the limitations which you create for yourself and for others before you have tested them out with facts and evidence. For example, believing that a person must know the status of every aspect of their job, at all times, warrants the following questions:

> **Ask more questions.**

- Why is that knowledge important?
- What would happen if he didn't know it?
- What would he be doing to acquire this knowledge?
- What evidence is there to prove this is what he must do?

Answers to these questions will reveal much about the believer's own experience and perceptions. Flexibility will increase if this leads to other options being generated.

Monitor the language you hear and allow yourself the choice to challenge anything which is disempowering – especially your own language. Develop a language which reduces need, and increases possibilities. Ask more questions. Approach situations in different ways, learning what works best and what does not work. Go against convention from time to time, test for relevancy and usefulness. And ask even more questions. Free yourself from the shackles of ritual and repetition.

> **Free yourself from the shackles of ritual and repetition.**

■ Eduction is the key to releasing potential

The process of eduction is crucial to the development of capability. It is a process of drawing out, rather than putting in. Galileo said 'You cannot teach a man anything, only help him discover it within himself.' This quotation reminds us of the importance of motivation in any development process – without the desire the will is weak. This is something which Nelson Mandela understands all too well from his experiences of educating his captors in the policies of the ANC. He knew that to force his ideas on his captors would invoke a defensive stance, so instead he would wait for them to ask him a question and work his teachings into the conversation as responses to their natural curiosity. Eduction is a

You cannot teach a man anything, only help him discover it within himself. [Galileo]

process that recognises these simple principles – the need for an inner desire to want to learn and develop, and the drawing out of ideas, answers, solutions and possibilities rather than putting in someone else's.

Blocks to eduction

- Short-term needs getting in the way of long-term development of potential.
- Negative beliefs about the capability people have to offer.
- Wanting to control others.
- Wanting to be the expert and teach others.
- Lack of skills needed for eduction.
- Too much emphasis on systems and procedures for business improvement.

Learning how to educt

The first thing to do is acquire the skills of a personal coach. There has been an increasing demand in business for coaching skills, mainly from management teams, and we see no reason why these superb skills should not be made available to everyone. Teams can coach one another – all you need is a healthy desire to learn and an understanding that it is the questions asked that are important, not who asks them. I frequently learn things from the questions my children ask as they challenge my perceptions of their world. In our business anyone can ask to be coached by anyone else, on any subject. The great thing about coaching is that you do not need to know very much about the subject to help someone work things out for himself. If, when interacting with others, you have at the front of your mind that your outcome is to leave the other person or team in control, that you want them to be able to do more, better, and that you want to kick-start a process of self-empowerment, your attitudes will be aligned with the purpose of eduction – to increase performance, and even more important than that, to develop capability for the future.

Eduction is not a natural human trait, it has to be learned. More natu-

Eduction is not a natural human trait, it has to be learned.

rally our human instinct prefers the role of advisor, instructor and proposer of solutions to people, working from the basis that our experience is useful to others. Often our experience is valuable to others, and so we should share it as an offer to be accepted with free will. But if you make this the mainstay of your support for people they will, of course, expect it whenever they get stuck. Our advice is to educt as a default strategy, drawing on experience and expert advice only as a back-up which should be made as an offer, never prescribed.

■ None of us is as smart as all of us

In our consulting experience we are sometimes asked to implement pre-planned development interventions, run a training event or design a course. The pre-planning has often been done by one or two line managers, perhaps with the help of the HR or training manager. This triggers alarm bells for us, because solutions so designed often prove to be flawed. In many of these cases, where we have been allowed to consult more widely, we have uncovered new information and new ideas from the people who are actually involved in the issues in question. Few organisations seem to afford the time necessary for an accurate diagnosis and needs analysis, keen to begin on planning and design. The Japanese proverb we have used as a title for this principle seems such an apt way of summarising this experience and stating a principle which we hold to be very valuable.

> Alignment activities encourage and strengthen team cohesion.

We introduced the metaphor of complicité in Chapter 8, and we explained how the actor, immersed in his character and delivering the script with animate conviction, must always be aware of, and engaged with, the other actors, and the audience. This sense of being an accomplice is crucial to the timing and overall synergy of the performance. Likewise in organisations, a sense of complicité helps build high performance teams. Alignment activities encourage and strengthen team cohesion.

It is often said that perception is everything, yet how easily we create false perceptions of what we think is happening around us. Collaborating as part of a team can help to purge false perceptions, giving individuals a clear view of the bigger picture and accurate representations of important details. The more a team knows about its individual members, the jobs they do, and their experiences the more synergy it will have.

Free to govern their own environment, and to make decisions on matters connected with their purpose teams can really begin to excel in their performance. Unfortunately, in our experience, overmanagement and underutilisation of teams is more common. If we want to realise the potential teams have to offer, a potential which is far greater than the sum of their numbers, they must be given the freedom to manage and direct themselves. Teams will be continuously realigning to various aspects of the business, sometimes adapting, other times shaping. Any team member or facilitator is ideally placed to coach the team in taking the responsibility for its own performance, and promoting the value of complicité.

Blocks to teamworking

Anything that reduces a team's freedom to choose how it is organised and aligned will act as a block. These five blocks are particularly effective at limiting a team's potential:

1 Doing too much for the team. Teams need a certain amount of support, but an overproviding manager or organisation can build dependency on external resources. It is better to encourage interdependence among team members, developing their networks for access to whatever resources they may need.
2 Experts and managers solving the team's problems for it. Give one solution and it will come back for another. This discourages the team from being creative and generating innovative solutions.
3 Managers withholding responsibility and authority by poor delegation skills.
4 Insufficient time allocated for team meetings.
5 An imbalance of priority between tasks, organisation and issues of alignment. It is as important to work *on* the team as it is to work *in* the team.

How to develop teamworking

Whether your role is team member, or team leader, your behaviour is open to interpretation by others. Team leaders will be formal role models for the team, carrying the weight of the organisation's authority. Others will be less formal role models. We all draw something from the behaviour we see around us. It is for this reason that, while the team leader's accountability may be greater than that of any one team member (this is not always the case), egalitarian relationships work best. Leading a team on this basis requires a certain dialogue, one that is more facilitative than directive or expert, and while we have introduced small bites of facilitative language in the book it is not feasible to represent the entire subject here. However, the language used by competent facilitators will help teams to become both egalitarian and effective. Here are some practical things a team can do to develop complicité.

- Share experiences openly, share feedback, and use it to do better. Learn how to take feedback positively, avoiding the defensiveness that prevents learning.
- Learn together. Put quality time aside for the team to learn from experience. Make this a priority structured process.
- Share details of individual roles. Improving each person's knowledge about the jobs others do in the team will make team support more effective.
- Hold rehearsals for projects.
- Ensure the team is involved in all stages of initiatives that affect them including:
  - diagnosis
  - decisions and designs
  - implementation
  - follow-up.
- Develop confidence and capability at all times by continuous learning, training and selecting challenging work assignments.
- Celebrate successes, be they small or large. From a smile and shake of the hand, to high fives and social events. Match the celebration to the success.

■ Be thorough and unrelenting with issues

One of our assignments involved a team whose members held a strong dislike for their manager. This was brought about by the manager's lack of people management skills. One of the consequences of this was a drop in the team's performance as it became increasingly dissatisfied with his management style. This had a noticeable effect on the ability to do a good job. For some months this obvious situation was overlooked while efforts to improve the team's performance were concentrated on the work it was doing. We think that we were given the brief because the CEO was either ignorant of the friction between them, or he didn't want to confront it.

Principles are only of use if the holder is committed to action. Words and intentions alone have little effect without the follow-through of action on the difficult issues that we have to face. It is relatively easy to suggest a different way of doing something compared to an issue concerning capability, values, beliefs or identity. But face up to these issues we must, in a thorough and relentless way, else we must be prepared to live with the consequences – and our conscience.

> **Principles are only of use if the holder is committed to action.**

Blocks to thoroughness

To the degree that we become enemies to the highest and best within us, do we become enemies to all. [Ralph W. Trine]

The greatest block is fear of confronting an issue because of the short-term consequences. We do not want to hurt people, or we may lack the confidence to make a direct approach to a colleague. We may not be able to muster the right words to use, or we may fear repercussions on ourself. If the issue is within us, perhaps an internal conflict of values, or an identity mismatch, we may have feelings of insecurity that prevent our facing the situation. Whatever the blocks that cause us to ignore the difficult issues, procrastination rarely helps, people just suffer in silence. This is where courage is needed.

How to be thorough and relentless

1 The place to begin work is with awareness. Learn how to recognise the difficult issues and understand their effect on people and the business. Listen for unclear purposes, identity problems and conflicts of values and beliefs. Capabilities are more difficult to spot – look for performance lower than past levels. Action is often the area of focus in most organisations, but an increased awareness of misalignments at the higher distinctions will reveal the true causes of poor performance.

2 Be outcome focused. Concentrate on purpose and the things to be achieved. Consider consequences. Avoid getting bogged down in personality traits. Use coaching skills to encourage self-appraisal and resolution. Discuss what is important for people and listen for belief statements. Use language that encourages options and difference, and be creative in the search for solutions.

3 Be courageous and committed to facing the big issues.

Learning to assimilate the principles

These eight principles may seem like common sense to some, and so once again we return to the fact that the simplest things are often the most difficult to learn – like respect, understanding and listening. Listening is one of the most sought-after skills in a large number of organisations, so we should not underestimate what is in involved in becoming a good listener. Assimilating these eight principles into everyday use is a matter of

> Assimilating these eight principles into everyday use is a matter of first, belief, and second, action.

first, belief, and second, action. If you believe that they will help your organisation to become more prosperous then you are well on your way to acquiring the necessary skills to make it happen. A highly effective way of developing the skills associated with the alignment principles is to form small action learning groups in the workplace, in conjunction with external workshops. Ideally, the management team will take on the belief and the learning will develop from that point.

The principles have been specifically selected to support an organisation's use of the universal alignment model. They have been distilled and crafted from the principles used by effective facilitators, business coaches, developers and leaders whom we have been privileged to work alongside. We have presented our version of those principles described in a way which matches our own experience. They should not be considered as an exclusive list, rather a minimum baseline of requirement for those engaged in alignment activities.

Used correctly, these principles will ensure that alignment actions win the commitment of the many, involving them in reshaping for the future and adapting processes of implementation. The result will be a common sharing of purpose, vision, values and beliefs that will unleash the true capability people have to offer. At the personal level individuals will make connections between organisational needs and their own needs and desires, learning a new language with which to balance the emotional and the intellectual domains. Some will find meaningful work adapting, while others will revel in the new opportunities to reshape the environment. The references for these changes will come not from a nucleus of thinkers, but from increasingly relevant feedback from the environment followed by intelligent responses from teams and individuals.

The picture we have painted is happening to differing degrees in a number of organisations. In our varied work we have helped organisations to achieve productivity gains in many different ways, but always as a result of working from the solid foundation of these eight principles, plus the courage and determination to help others succeed. The future is not what it used to be – so let's shape it together.

index

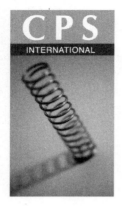

'Creatively developing the human resource'

Alignment programmes

Addressing the key themes of successful organisations our programmes build the commitment for alignment through assimilation of the eight principles of purposeful change. The eight principles are a common theme in all our alignment activities.

■ Aligning the organisation

This programme is designed with the client to ensure that all aspects of the organisation are included, and that the client is involved in deciding the scope, timing and content of the programme. In helping an organisation to adopt alignment we are very much facilitators of the client's own thinking processes.

Typically this option will consist of a range of activities including facilitating workshops, coaching teams, personal coaching for significant role models, and in some cases training courses. The outcome is to leave clients fully capable of perpetuating alignment for themselves.

■ Aligning teams

No two teams are the same, they differ in many ways. Our approach to helping teams become aligned begins by recognising and respecting individual attitudes and capabilities. We meet you where you are and facilitate your transition to becoming a high performance team. Using a mix of indoor and outdoor activities team alignment programmes are built together with the team members. They can be organised for a single team, or for multiple teams wanting to improve the effectiveness of interteam co-operation.

■ Leadership alignment

Effective leadership is the key to unlocking potential. Aligning a consistent style of leadership with the purpose of the organisation provides a solid foundation for further development. From here the eight principles will help to build desired leadership behaviours that work to stretch the capabilities of individuals every day. Effective leaders are themselves aligned with a strong sense of personal purpose – and this is where we begin, creating and strengthening leadership within so that you can enable leadership without.

■ Pathways to innovation

Our Pathways offering is tailored to each client and may consist of a wide range of activities. Typically, we will support you in getting the climate right for innovation, building creative teams, stimulating creative thinking and designing an innovation delivery system.

For more information about Alignment in practice contact:

CPS International
Oxford: +44 (0) 1865 715 895
Frodsham: +44 (0) 1928 734 333
Fax: +44 (0) 1928 739 717
Email: innovate@cpsinter.com
Website: www.cpsinter.com